Publications Committee
Faculty of Education
Memorial University of Newfoundland
St. John's, Newfoundland
A1B 3X8

1995

ISBN: 0-88901-276-8

ii

SCHOOL HUMOUR:

PEDAGOGICAL AND SOCIOLOGICAL

CONSIDERATIONS

Wilfred B.W. Martin
Ishmael J. Baksh

i

TABLE OF CONTENTS

PART I

ORIENTATIONS AND METHODS

PART II

STUDENT VIEWS ON SCHOOL HUMOUR
IN ATLANTIC CANADA

PART III

CLASSROOM OBSERVATIONS

PREFACE

Despite the research focus on the structure and process of schooling over the years, the complexities of the culture of this microcosm of society are not fully understood. The aim of this book is to add to our appreciation of one dimension of interactions in this setting -- school humour. Specifically, this is a sociological study of school humour with the twin aims of identifying pedagogical dimensions of humour and pinpointing concepts and issues that need to be addressed as one moves toward the development of a sociological theory of classroom humour.

This book is designed for teachers, high school teachers in particular, who are interested in the student perspective of school humour and the functions of classroom humour; and for prospective teachers as they study the processes of teaching, learning, classroom management and interpersonal relations in general.

The first part of this book is devoted to a review of earlier writings on school humour and to a description of the methodology used in the present study of humour in teacher-student and student-student interactions in high schools of Atlantic Canada. Drawing on students' comments relating to school climate, joking in the classroom, individual and group processes in humour, and the social-emotional dimensions of classroom humour, their views of school humour are presented in considerable detail the second part of this book. The context and form of classroom humour are illustrated in the third part of this book with episodes of humour recorded during classroom observations. The final part of the book focuses on the practice and theory of classroom humour.

The co-operation of school boards, principals, teachers and high students in Atlantic Canada is hereby acknowledged. This study could not have done without their assistance, and we are truly grateful to them. Given our commitment to anonymity, those people are not identified in this publication. Any names included by way of describing particular classroom situations are fictitious.

PART I

ORIENTATIONS AND METHODS

Traditionally, there was a widely held view that humour and laughter were frivolous activities that had no place in the classroom. Teaching with a sense of humour was seen as unprofessional by teachers at all levels of formal education; high school teachers and college instructors in particular avoided the use of humour because of the seriousness they associated with their tasks.

Despite the long standing view that the educational process, particularly within organizations such as colleges and schools, is gloomy and lifeless, there is a growing realization that humour can be of substantial importance in promoting teaching and learning. In fact, there has been a considerable amount of research illustrating the pedagogical advantages of humour, particularly at the school level (primary, elementary and secondary) and demonstrating that humour permeates interactions and teaching strategies in many classrooms. Part I of this book reviews the research which focuses on school humour, outlines the theoretical orientation on which the present study is based and presents the data collection techniques employed in the present study of school humour in Atlantic Canada.

CHAPTER 1

A LITERATURE REVIEW

Observations show that humour is employed, in varying degrees, by people at different levels of the school organization. Given that schools have at least three overlapping organizational dimensions (that is, bureaucratic, professional, and curriculum), as well as particular physical arrangements (for example, staffrooms and classrooms), it is not surprising to find that organizational positions and physical location have been addressed in the study of school humour. The present review of the literature on school humour focuses on humour and school administrators, humour in school counselling, staffroom humour, and classroom humour. Finally, the chapter notes the focus of the research reported on in this book.

Humour and School Administrators

Although this review of the literature relating to school humour did not identify any research on the extent and nature of humour among school administrators, one study (Ziegler, Boardman and Thomas, 1985) addressed the issues of when leaders can utilize humor to increase their effectiveness and how leaders can use humour to be more effective. Another publication (Dardick, 1990) offered practical advice for reducing frustrations in the role of the principal.

Viewing humour in the context of facilitating and enhancing the communication between superordinate and subordinates, and of lessening hostility and creating a relaxed atmosphere, Ziegler, Boardman and Thomas (1985) argue that humour

3

has the potential of being an extremely useful tool for school administrators. In their study

of humour, leadership and school climate, these writers identified five categories of humour:

> Neat, Light-hearted -- Jokes stress, shorter, light-hearted retort
> of a snappy tone.
> Cheerful Independence -- Jokes have a general tone of
> cheerfulness and acceptance.
> Damaging Retort -- Jokes tend toward preponderance of
> damaging, hostile come-backs against life or custom in general.
> Rebound Against Feminine Aggression -- Jokes are directed
> against women largely in terms of their naivete or foolishness.
> Dullness -- Jokes involve limited subtlety and verbal, ability.
> (Ziegler, Boardman and Thomas, 1985:347).

They found that there was a significant positive correlation between neat light-

hearted humour and cheerful independence, on the one hand, and leadership which is

concerned about the comfort, well-being and contributions of subordinates, on the other.

There was a significant negative correlation between damage retort humour and this

particular aspect of leadership. While there was a significant positive correlation between

cheerful independence humour and school climate (that is, the administrative environment of

the school as created by the policies and practices of the top administrators), dullness humour

was negatively correlated with school climate.

The potential for being frustrated in their jobs is common knowledge among

principals. Humour has been identified as having the potential of playing an important role

in dealing with the stresses of the job. In his "laughing works seminars", Dardick (1990)

offered a number of suggestions for adding laughter to the principal's day. To paraphrase

these suggestions, (1) instead of resenting your alarm when you wake up in the morning try

thinking of it as an opportunity alert; (2) use props to create chuckles; (3) when faced by a

tough problem ask yourself how your favourite comedian would deal with it; (4) instead of fuming when you put the phone on hold, have a book of cartoons nearby to look at; (5) have baby pictures of yourself and your staff members displayed on a prominent bulletin board; (6) create an office humour file with jokes from magazines and newspapers; (7) make fun of yourself in front of others; (8) carry a humour first-aid kit in your briefcase, perhaps including in it a mask, outrageous glasses or whatever you think will make your staff members laugh; (9) to deal with chronic complainers on your staff, institute a policy that complaints must be put to music and sung; and (10) develop your own style of humour based on the "A.T.T. Rule of Comedy". Such a style must be appropriate, timely and tasteful. In sum, the suggestion is that these tactics could help decrease the tensions associated with the roles of school administrators, and could take the edge of potentially depressing situations. Obviously, some of these suggestions are more suited to the overall orientations of certain principals than of others.

"Parental excuses" are the only examples that Dardick gives of what makes principals laugh. Such excuses include:

> The basement of our house got flooded where the children slept so they had to be evaporated.

> Please excuse Connie from gym class today, as she had difficulty breeding.

> Anne did not do her homework because I couldn't understand it.

If this is the only, or even the predominant, form of humour for the school principal, it may be seen as a reflection of the position itself and of the general nature of school culture. One could query whether the adage that it is lonely at the top is applicable to the school environment. The research on staffroom humour, as discussed below, shows that the school bureaucracy and administrators are the butt of much of the humour amongst teachers in this setting. As indicated in the review of the writings on classroom humour later in this chapter and in the findings of the present study of school humour presented in subsequent chapters, a considerable portion of student humour is enacted in relation to the teacher, the position directly above the students in the bureaucratic line of authority.

Humour in School Counselling

The significance of the role of humour in therapy and counselling has received considerable attention from a number of perspectives (e.g., Cousins, 1980; 1989; Chapman and Foot, 1977). Goodman suggested that counsellors should develop a comic vision, concentrate on looking for humour in situations, and take notes on everything that strikes them as funny to help reinforce humour in their lives (Crabbs, Crabbs and Goodman, 1986:106). One study (Zingler 1985) outlined six constructive functions of humour in counselling: humour as healer, humour as reframer, humour as creativity, humour as relationship builder, humour as fun, and humour as therapy. Empathy, acceptance and genuineness were seen to be core factors in promoting constructive humour. The destructive functions of humour were identified by viewing humour as aggression, humour as superiority, humour as defense mechanism, and humour as social distance.

Focusing specifically on the role of the school counsellor, different writers have argued that there is a need to understand the various dimensions of humour as identified by psychologists and psychotherapists. These dimensions have been referred to as the distinction between producing and appreciating humour (Kuhlman, 1984), or developing and

6

applying humour (Goodman, 1983) or creative humour and appreciative humour (Ziv, 1984).

For Ziv (1984:111) creative humour is

> ...the ability to perceive relationships between people, objects,
> or ideas in an incongruous way, as well as the ability to
> communicate this perception to others. This communication
> may be verbal and elicits in others smile or laughter.

Appreciative humour is

> ...the ability to understand and enjoy messages containing
> humor creativity, as well as situations that are incongruous but
> not menacing.

Sluder (1986:121) illustrates the interrelatedness between creative and

appreciative humour with the following examples:

> ... a third-grade teacher received a complaint from a student that
> one of his classmates had bitten him. Examining the
> outstretched hand and finding no evidence of injury, the teacher
> replied, 'Did you ask if he'd had his rabies shot?' The two
> boys laughed and went off to play together. She created; they
> appreciated.
>
> The student who hides a rubber snake in the teacher's desk
> drawer is creating humor. The teacher who laughingly pulls it
> out by the tail is appreciating the humor. The teacher is
> modeling and encouraging humorous behavior while keeping
> classroom management in it proper perspective.

According to Sluder (1986), humour is an important element in the elementary

school counsellor's role. To elaborate, she argued that the counsellor's role includes: (1)

cultivating a school atmosphere that is conducive to creative and appreciative humour; (2)

encouraging teachers to incorporate humour into formal classroom learning experiences; (3)

employing humour as a disciplinary strategy, e.g., establishing rapport and defusing anger

and tension; (4) modelling a good sense of humour; (5) scheduling group guidance classes

7

for nurturing and developing humour, e.g., use of literature with humorous characters and role playing; and (6) incorporating humour informally in small group and individual counselling.

In addition to having a sense of humour to facilitate one's work with students, different writers have pointed to the need for school counsellors to have a sense of humour for the sake of their own well-being. Leone (1986:140-141), for example, suggested a variety of ways in which school counsellors might laugh and thereby relieve the stress associated with their profession. In point form they are: (1) enjoy your work -- fill your office with things you enjoy; (2) stop lying to yourself -- if you are not happy don't try to fool yourself in thinking you are happy, do something about it; (3) expand your range of activities; (4) dare to be a 'nerd' at times; (5) use role playing -- do things you may not like because you are not good at them by pretend to be someone who can do them well; (6) find a favourite comic -- listen to a humorous tape, see a comedy movie, learn a joke or two; (7) use humorous anecdotes and examples; and (8) restructure your day --change your routine, learn what your students think is funny.

Staffroom Humour

To even a casual observer it is obvious that talk is one of the major activities in the staffroom. Undoubtedly, a number of factors, including happenings within the teaching profession itself as well as events in the community and societal arenas and on the international stage as reported through mass media, influence its content. While not the focus of the present research, our observations in staffrooms over the years have led us to suggest that issues relating to students' academic performances and lifestyles dominate

8

staffroom talk. The significance of teachers' talk within the staffroom as a means of creating group solidarity among teachers is seen in an early anthropological study of American schools (Fuchs, 1969) and later sociological studies in Newfoundland (Stebbins, 1975) and Britain (Hammersley, 1981; 1984).

Woods (1984) identified laughter as the most prominent feature of staffroom relationships. He described the staffroom as "a haven in stormy seas" where teachers are often on the lookout for laughter as a means of finding relief from conflict and frustration experienced in the school. The bureaucratic nature of the school itself and administrators who are perceived to be over zealous in their adherence to institutionalized structures were the most common topics in initiating staffroom humour. However, Woods (1984:196) also observed that, on occasions, humour developed "out of nothing in particular". As such, it can be seen as "a creative act ... a growth experience".

The influence of bureaucratic characteristics of schooling on staffroom humour is also implicit in the observation that joking relationships thrive among teachers in schools characterized by formal classrooms (Goodson and Walker, 1991). The staffroom is the obvious arena for these relationships to be nurtured. It is the one place in the school where teachers' talk is not accessible to students and generally not overheard by administrators. In line with this, Woods (1990:200) observed that the "solidarity humour" of the staffroom protects teachers from attacks on their teaching identities. Tacking jokes and cartoons to the staffroom bulletin board may contribute to cohesiveness among teachers (Clifton and Roberts, 1993:5-6).

9

It is possible that the nature of staffroom humour is, in one way or another, a continuation of humour which teachers employed while they were studying to become teachers. For example, Mealyea's (1989) study of tradespeople who were studying to become teachers revealed that humour was used as a coping strategy by these student-teachers when they were faced with a substantive threat to their occupational self-identity. It is speculated that prospective teachers from other backgrounds employ humour at different times and for various reasons during their educational careers leading to their becoming teachers. If humour is part of the socialization processes in becoming a teacher, it will continue to be a part of the developing teacher identities within the staffroom.

Classroom Humour

Among the issues identified in the literature as pertinent to different dimensions of classroom humour are (1) the social-psychological development of children and the accompanying development in humour appreciation and expression, (2) the formal versus informal nature of classroom structure, and (3) the role of language in classroom humour. After addressing these issues, this review of the literature notes studies on each of four topics: (1) class clowns, (2) subject specific humour, (3) humour and test performance, and (4) functions of classroom humour. Finally, potential dangers of teacher initiated classroom humour are noted.

A Development View

Within the tradition of Piaget and other structural developmentalists, researchers (e.g., Krogh, 1986; McGhee 1974a; 1974b; 1976; McGhee and Chapman, 1980) have highlighted a developmental approach to the study of humour among children, with

10

particular attention to the childhood years. Briefly, the argument is that as individuals progress from one stage of development to the next a transformation takes place in both the way they view the world and the concepts they hold for it. As summarized by Tamashiro (1979:70) the types of humour associated with each stage of development are presented in Table 1-1.

TABLE 1-1

STAGES OF DEVELOPMENT AND TYPES OF HUMOR

Stage	Type of Humor
Pre-social/Symbolic (Infant)	Tickling, body contact
Impulsive	Physical-body functions, clowning, slapstick humor, nonsense expressions, chanting
Self-protective	Practical jokes, insults, hostile humor
Conformist	Conventional jokes, riddles, word plays, moron jokes, racial-ethnic humor
Conscientious (later adolescence or adulthood)	Original, good-natured humor, tongue-in-cheek humor, social satire

Several points have been advanced concerning the application of the development view for classroom teachers. For example, in developing classroom management strategies and in selecting disciplinary measures, it is important for teachers to have an understanding of the general developmental levels of their students and the types of humour associated with these levels. Also, children's expressions of humour might be encouraged as a means of stimulating cognitive and personal development.

11

Formal and Informal Classrooms

The extent to which humour is present in the classroom is undoubtedly related to the nature of the social relationships in this setting. Ziv (1984) found that a democratic atmosphere spawns more humour than an authoritarian one. Goodson and Walker (1991:1-43) make a distinction between "formal" and "informal" classrooms. The formal classroom is one where the teacher is constantly "on stage" to the entire class. That is, everyone in the classroom is in the audience or the potential audience. The teacher is always in control of those present. Classroom organization and the social identity of the teacher in the classroom are two of the main ingredients of the control process in this setting. The teacher's social identity in the classroom is seen to be different from his/her identity outside of this environment.

In contrast to the central and controlling nature of the teacher's presence in the formal classroom, the teacher's presence in the informal classroom is less visible. In fact, the teacher in such a situation may go unnoticed by many of the students present. A considerable proportion of a teacher's time is spent speaking to students individually or in small groups. Classroom organization, rather than teacher identity, is the dominant dimension of control in the informal classroom. In this type of a classroom, the teacher has more a personal identity than a positional one. That is to say, the teacher is seen to be the same type of person within and outside the classroom.

Goodson and Walker (1991:7-27) argued that since communication is more focused and centralized in the formal than in the informal classroom, the formal classroom is more conducive to the telling of "jokes" than the latter. In such classrooms the teacher takes

12

of a "joker". Rather than taking the role of joker and developing the accompanying

however, teachers in the informal classroom tend to develop joking relationships

students as the basis of humour in the classroom. Joking relationships are

n situation comedy and are more free flowing than relationships built around telling

ey are also without the clearly defined boundaries usually associated with joke

telling. By way of summarizing their observations on humour in the classroom, Goodson

and Walker (1991:43) offer "connecting hypotheses," including the following:

1. Classrooms exhibit different forms of humour, the forms indicating differences in situational structure. Formal situations generate jokes: informal situations engender comedy.

2. This distinction involves different forms of teacher-pupil relationships. The formal classroom situation creates roles as jokers. The informal situation rends to create joking relationships between teacher and pupil.

3. Joking relationships between pupils thrive in predominantly formal situations, but tend to be expressed primarily outside the classroom and are often inaccessible to teachers.

4. Jokes between teachers and pupils frequently function to negotiate the framing of educational knowledge (in Bernstein's sense). Teacher's jokes are often bids for social control; pupil jokes (to the teacher) are frequently challenges to that control.

Class Clowns

After 3,500 eighth grade students identified 96 class clowns, most of whom

were males, from among their ranks, Damico and Purkey (1978) found that teachers saw the

clowns to be higher than those who were not clowns in assertiveness, unruliness, attention

seeking, leadership and cheerfulness, and lower than others in achievement. They also found

that class clowns, compared to others, had less favourable attitudes toward their teacher and

13

principal. However, the clowns perceived themselves to be leaders and open in expressing their ideas and opinions in front of their classmates. Later, Damico (1980:133) made an important distinction between the role of the whimsical clown and that of the hostile clown in the classroom. The latter is disruptive to the teaching-learning process and a liability to the overall well-being of the classroom. In contrast, students who engage in clowning/whimsical humour often make positive contributions to a more desirable classroom structure. From her sociometric study of adolescent class clowns, Damico suggested that whimsical class clowns can release tensions within the classroom, increase a sense of group cohesion among the students, and convey students' feelings and attitudes that would not otherwise become known to teachers. Among the challenges facing teachers with respect to class clowns are the tasks of distinguishing between the two types of clowns (two types of humour) and of taking steps necessary to help the hostile clown while maximizing the benefits to be gained from the whimsical clown's actions.

Language and Humour

While there may be a range of social, psychological, temporal and physical characteristics influencing the perception of what is humorous at a given time, the ambiguity of language is often an important source of humour in everyday life. The potential for humour in the multiple levels of meanings in words has been noted by Hill (1988:57-61) to be associated with homonyms (words that sound the same but differ in spelling and meanings, for example, "hole" and "whole"), puns (a play on words), oxymoron (opposite terms that seem to contradict each other, for example, "poor millionaire"), redundancy (unnecessary repetitiveness) and incorrect word order (for example, "one unanswered

14

question is the author of the book"). Also, as discussed by Hill (1988: 65), cliches are among the conventions found in language based humour (for example, "If I told you once, I've told you a hundred times"), as are metaphors (for example, "you are in the spring of life"). Using colloquial language in the formal setting of the classroom may also be a source of humour.

Subject Specific Humour

Starting with his observations that the school literary magazine developed by the seventh and eighth grade students in a school he observed in the United States had nothing humorous in it, Weiss (1981) argued that humour has a serious application in the field of English. Writers have used exaggerations and absurdities for seemingly opposing purposes, that is, to make people laugh and to increase social consciousness through thinking about human values and behaviour. Richard Armour, a teacher of English for more than forty years, claims that the use of pun and parody can be successfully employed in teaching English. He suggests that, if there were such a thing as a "Humor Quotient", it would be close to the "Intelligent Quotient" in that the better-than-average students would "get it" and simultaneously laugh and learn quicker than the average and below average students (Armour, 1975). It has been observed that humour draws teenagers to sophisticated books where they get enjoyment from allusion and parodies, from the gross and anti-poetic and from seeing the world beyond their immediate environments (Nilsen and Nilsen, 1982).

One writer (Keenan, 1985), as an example of how teachers can add humour to the teaching of economics, suggested an imaginative dialogue between Karl Marx and Adam

Smith debating who should own MacDonald's chain of restaurants and whether designer jeans should be produced .

While arguing that physics can be fun when the concepts and applications of the subject are approached with a sense of humour, Ivars Peterson, a physics teacher in Ontario at the time, offered a number of suggestions for teaching this subject. He observed that a good starting point is using cartoons to add humour to the classroom. In less than five years, Peterson collected several hundred cartoons that he used to illustrate important points, to introduce topics and to indicate common misconceptions in physics. Peterson goes on to suggest that the use of puns (verbal and visual) can be a very effective way of getting students' attention and giving them the satisfaction of showing how clever they are. Decorating the classroom with posters that have humorous overtones to them and turning the lesson into a game show are also offered as ways of inserting humour into the physics lesson. By way of conclusion, Peterson (1981: 649-650) wrote that, to be an effective teacher, the physics teacher does not need to be a comedian, continually cracking jokes, inventing puns and tossing off one-liners. A happy and creative atmosphere can be generated through the judicious use of humour in the classroom.

One physics teacher (Adams, 1972) illustrated how he used humour while examining how well students learned the subject at hand. He inserted humour into tests by developing items around current events or problems, and by fitting the names of current physics students and situations into the tests. On the basis of his experiences with these strategies, he argued that the only thing that humour on physics tests distracts students from is "nervousness".

Humour and Test Performance

Considerable attention has been given to the effects of humour on creativity in general and on test scores in particular subjects over the years. For example, Ziv (1976) investigated the influence of listening to humour and scores on creativity tests of 282 tenth grade students. Operationalizing creativity as scores on a creativity test, Ziv found that laughter response to humorous stimuli increases creative thinking in adolescents. Ziv's (1986) later studies of the influence of a humorous atmosphere on students' creativity scores also found that a humorous atmosphere significantly increases creativity scores.

As noted above, Adams (1972) reported that the use of humour in test items improved the test performance of high school physics students. Arguing that the introduction of humour into testing situations can help relax the anxiety level of students, Smith et al. (1971) concluded that humour can facilitate their test performances.

When comparing the performances of third and fifth grade students who worked on a humorous test with that of students who worked on a test that was not humorous, Terry and Woods (1975) found that humour depressed the performances of third graders, and had both positive and negative effects on the performances of fifth graders. From this study of the test performance of students in one low socio-economic neighbourhood school in the United States, they concluded that the effects of humour on test performance "are mediated by the momentary arousal levels of students".

With eighth-grade English classes as their sample, McMorris, Urbach and Connor (1985) incorporated humour into grammar test items and administered them to 126 students from six classes as they sought answers to three questions: (1) Does performance on

17

a humorous form of a test differ from performance on a nonhumorous form? (2) Does the inclusion of humor in test items affect students' anxiety level? (3) What do students perceive as the effects of humor on their test performance? Their conclusions were that inclusion of humorous items on the test did not affect grammar scores on matched humorous/nonhumorous items or on common post-treatment items, and they did not affect the current anxiety level of the students. While the humorous items did not affect test performance or anxiety level, students favoured the inclusion of such items on tests. However, another study of the relationship between humour and competence in children between the ages of 10 and 14 found that humour is positively related to competence, those measures of competence including teacher ratings of classroom behaviour, peer reputation and achievement (Masten, 1986).

While there is not a consensus on the issue of whether humour enhances the retention of subject matter, there is widespread agreement that humour enhances the learning experience. The argument is that humour shows the human side of teachers and creates a sense of humanity in the classroom.

Functions of Classroom Humour

In a book titled Beyond Laughter, published almost forty years ago, Grotjahn (1957) suggested that laughter enhanced learning. Nine years later Eble (1966), in his book on The Perfect Education, argued that humour opens up pathways to creativity and discovery. Focusing specifically on the classroom, Armour (1975:61) expressed a desire to see more humour in the classroom and more recognition of humour as a teaching aid. While suggesting that too much humour can be disastrous, Armour argued for its use "as a bit of

18

dessert, an intellectual reward". Rogers (1984:46) also opined that "laughter is far to rare in today's classroom". He complained:

> Our obsession with effectiveness and efficiency, time-on-task, standards, discipline, skills, objectives, inputs, outputs, test scores, fear, and failure have turned schools into rather grim places.

Rogers goes on to suggest that teachers and students alike need a "humorous outlook" for humour to become a meaningful part of the schooling experience. In a similar vein, Mindess (1971) observed that a humorous frame of mind, which is considered as a prerequisite for nurturing humour in any setting, is characterized by flexibility, spontaneity, unconventionality, shrewdness, playfulness and humility. In other words, interactions in the school are to be flexible, spontaneous, unconventional, playful and humble.

From her review of research on classroom humour, Hill (1988:20-24) listed eight functions of humour in this setting. First, humour can create a positive learning environment. Second, it may enhance the retention of subject matter. Third, humour may be a form of education in itself in that by relating jokes to each other students inevitably pass on knowledge. Fourth, humour is believed to promote "physical well-being and mental health" in the classroom, thereby helping students deal with the stress associated with teaching and learning. Fifth, humour is often seen as an acceptable way for students to protest their perception of their lack of power and control in the classroom. Sixth, there is an "appeasement function of humour" in that it often makes light of an issue that is otherwise seen as serious within the setting. Seventh, humour may function as a "coping mechanism"; it is a forum whereby students share their personal problems with one another. Eighth, humour can function as a distancing mechanism as it arises in crisis situations. That is to

19

say, students joke about a crisis as a way of distancing themselves from experiencing the pain associated with it.

A number of interrelated points can be made by way of summarizing the research relating to the functions of classroom humour. It has been found that humour can be an important ingredient in creating a positive learning environment. Also, humour is an important part of communication between teachers and students, as well as among the students. Given the authority/power relationships between teachers and students, a certain amount of tension is inevitable in the classroom. Humour may be seen as a socially acceptable way of expressing the frustration experienced in this setting. It has also been demonstrated that student learning can be reinforced with humorous associations. To elaborate further, a review of the literature on the functions of classroom humour reveals that there has been research on the functions of teacher humour as well as the functions of student humour.

Teacher Initiated Humour

In 1932, a time when teachers were often known for their lack of humour and for their authoritarian approach to classroom management, Willard Waller (1965:229-230) observed:

> There are some teachers who think that they should never smile.
> They may be right, for where the moral order is frankly
> imposed upon students from without they will welcome any
> show of relaxation on the part of the imposing agent as an
> opportunity to break though. Teachers who never smile,
> however, lose an opportunity to gain status as human beings, for
> the thought that after all 'Old So-and-So' has no sense of humor
> or 'knows how to take a joke' is one which makes students less
> inimical and teacher domination less unbearable.

20

Almost four decades after Waller's observation on humour in teaching, Carl Rogers (1969), in his widely acclaimed book on Freedom to Learn, noted that a sense of humour is one of the essential qualities of good teachers. Others have pursued this line of thought and have offered advice to those who want to become humour conscious teachers. For example, Vincent Rogers (1984:48-49) suggests that such teachers (1) are prepared to share their mistakes and laugh at themselves, (2) encourage students to see the inconsistencies in their behaviour, to laugh at themselves and to release tension while in the classroom, (3) teach children not to laugh at ethnic jokes, (4) find ways to show films by comic artists, (5) display pictures and posters of comic artists, (6) ask students to keep humour diaries or journals, to make list of favourite jokes, to do humour surveys, (7) and encourage students to observe what makes people laugh. The underlining argument is that school is not only a preparation for life but is life itself. Hence, the emotions, including laughing, that are a part of being human in contemporary North American, Canadian and Newfoundland cultures should have a place in the school environment as well.

From observations of classroom humour in Newfoundland schools, Stebbins (1980:86-87) suggested that humour serves the function of comic relief most frequently at the end of the school day and toward the end of the school week. Focusing on different types of social interactions in the school, Woods (1983) argued that humour acts as either a facilitator of harmonious relationship or as resistance to discord. To elaborate, Woods suggested that the facilitator role is evident where joking forms a cultural bond between teacher and student. Teachers and students come to give a joint definition of the situation and simultaneously making an alliance against differences in authority and status. The role of teacher humour in

21

resisting discord is seen as teachers react to the bureaucratic and inhuman dimensions of school life.

Walker and Goodson (1977: 206-207) noted contrasting functions of teacher humour. On the one hand, teachers often joke in order to show that they are in control. The argument is that teachers need a strong sense of being in control before letting jokes play a central role in their teaching. Under such circumstances, teachers may successfully employ self-disparaging jokes. On the other hand, as Walker and Goodson reported, a teacher might use jokes to expose his/her own weakness in making things stick in the classroom. As illustrated in Willis' (1977) ethnographic study of male white working class counter-school culture, self-disparaging jokes in positions of weakness may undermine the little control which the teacher has. Teachers have been known to initiate humour as a means of recognizing the defects of schooling, the bureaucratic presence and the inhuman structures that permeate the teaching-learning environment.

Teachers may use jokes to bypass the impersonal dimensions of the organizational domain of the school and thereby make an alliance with the students on a personal level. In other words, teachers take a distance from the more formal aspects of their role to create and foster informal relationships with the students. It is suspected that teachers who use humour in this way are seen to be among the friendliest teachers in the school, where friendliness is viewed as a positive characteristic in teacher-student relationships (Martin, 1983:67-77).

In addition to suggesting the desirability of encouraging teachers to develop and employ a sense of humour in their interactions with students, some writers have advocated giving teachers actual instructions on how to use humour. One such instructional

package was developed by Parsons (1977) at the University of Alberta. Ziv (1983) found

that such instructions were instrumental in fostering creativity, and he concluded that they

would have positive results on the overall atmosphere of the classroom.

Student Initiated Humour

There are many reasons why students initiate humour. Such humour comes in

many forms and has a multitude of consequences social relationships in the school. To begin

this review of the research on student humour, it is noted that classroom humour has been

categorized as to whether it is unintentional or intentional. The unintentional forms include

bloopers, stumbles, accidents and private jokes. Stebbins (1980:92) wrote that a blooper is

"an involuntary wording blemish, such as an unwilling substitution of a word for the

intended one, or a reversal of two or more words", while a stumble is an "involuntary

stammering or the momentary inability to enunciate a sentence as the speaker would like".

Classroom accidents which may been seen as humorous include such things as dropping a

book, writing so the chalk makes a squeaking noise on the board or breaking a piece of chalk

on the board. Private jokes, that is in-group student jokes, may occur when something the

teacher says has humorous connotations that the teacher is unaware of but attracts the

attention of students.

Intentional classroom humour has been observed to include "witticisms, antics,

funning, practical jokes, narrative jokes and sporting put-ons" (Stebbins, 1980;92). The

following example of witticism as expressed through a wisecrack and a put-down is from

Stebbins' (1975:113) research in Newfoundland classrooms:

23

Students were arriving late that morning, as a result of a minor snowstorm that slowed the flow of traffic through the city. Mr. Simms, one of the high school mathematics teachers, said almost nothing to his latecomers, since he understood their problem that morning and since there were instructions from the Vice-Principal to admit them directly into class. But when Stan walked through the door thirty-five minutes after the period began, Mr. Simms waxed cynical. 'Why are we so honoured this morning?' he inquired. Stan paused for a moment and then retorted: 'If you don't want me to come, I'll leave.' The class laughed. As he made his way to his desk, Mr. Simms made a further comment about the snow in Stan's driveway, and with more laughter from the rest of the students resumed discussion of mathematical symbols. When interviewed approximately an hour later, the teacher was still in a censorious mood over Stan's late arrival. 'He had spent many days in the detention room (for being late),' he observed. 'He was planning on staying away (today), but it was snowing... and he would have had to shovel... It was the easiest way out to come to school...' Yet, Stan and Mr. Simms generally seemed to have a cordial relationship; Mr. Simms believed he was seen as pleasant and fair enough to be attractive to this student.

Here is an example of classroom antics reported by Stebbins' (1980:93):

Mrs. Baxter was making the rounds to those of her pupils in need of help with the seat work assignment. She taught in a traditional self-contained classroom, within which several ranks of desks were separated by aisles scarcely wide enough to allow student movement. Consequently, her rather portly frame, which nearly touched the desks on either side as she manoeuvred up the passageway, virtually pushed Anne, who was behind her, to the other side of her desk when she (the teacher) bent over to assist one of her classmates. For Anne the opportunity was irresistible. After quietly getting the attention of those nearby, she aimed a pair of compasses at the teacher's plump backsides, swung, and stopped within an inch of the unlikely target. Sniggering broke the studious quiet of the room. Annoyed, Mrs. Baxter whirled and scowled in the direction from which it came, though she had no idea of its cause.

A study of students in a comprehensive school in South Wales suggests that they engaged in what was known as "sussing out" teachers. They used a range of humour strategies (risque jokes, lavatorial humour, repartee and wit, and private jokes) to identify the teacher perspective of schooling including teachers' views on methods of teaching and control. This knowledge was important for them as they proceeded to develop a student culture (Beynon, 1979 as reported in Woods, 1983:114). Put differently, the students wanted to test the waters as they developed their own culture within the classroom.

One British study (Pollard, 1979:88) reported that students joke with their teachers in order to have fun, and on occasions, teachers are willing participants in such actions. "Intrinsic as opposed to subversive enjoyment" is often a dominant characteristic of those situations. In those and other classroom situations, humour is contagious. For example, Denscombe (1980) observed that a private joke may spread quickly among the students in open classrooms in comprehensive schools. Humour has also been observed to provide a "legitimate respite from the rigours of work" (Denscombe, 1980:64).

Adolescent girls observed by Ransoholf (1975) told anecdotes and jokes that focused on physical changes during puberty. This sexual humour served two functions: to relieve anxieties about developmental concerns and to enhance group cohesion. Woods (1983) illustrated his proposal that humour is a way for students to express their resistance to school structure by drawing on Willis' (1977) report of students who resisted the impositional forces of the school, and on Corrigan's (1979) study of schools as settings of power. From Corrigan's research it is suggested that humour and the accompanying laughter are student strategies for coping with school life. This is exemplified in students "mucking about" in the classroom. The underlying reason for student resistance is frequently the development and protection of self in its relationship to others in the school.

25

Highlighting the coping function of humour and laughter, Woods (1990:194) has argued that much of the student humour that he, and others, have observed in British schools has "to do with their own personal development, experimenting with identities, and the social formation of the groups to which they belong." To elaborate, it has been found that nicknames student's have for one another promote solidarity in the group (Woods, 1990:196-197). An observational study of students in a boys' comprehensive school in South Wales found that violence itself, as well as the resultant punishment from teachers, provided laughter among the boys, and that such laughter contributed to the formation of one's self-esteem.

Woods (1990:200-205) has also argued that laughter is sometimes used to promote and defend school rules that are designed to govern student behaviour. Teachers and students laugh together as the students cope with the rules that are beyond their and teachers' control, in this way creating a joint definition of the situation as well as distancing themselves from the situation. At other times, teachers and students are in opposition to each other and student humour is in conflict with the expectation of the teachers. Together they search for, they negotiate, acceptable patterns of interaction in the situation at hand.

An experimental study of elementary school children in the United States found that males who displayed hostile humour did not engage in much social play with their peers (McGhee, 1976). The suggestion is that such children do not feel a part of the in-group structure of the classroom. Related to the notion of hostile behaviour is that of "mucking around". One observational study of British students noted that mucking around in the classroom include such behaviours as

> ... twanging rulers, shining mirrors, misappropriating school
> furniture and equipment, scuffing with neighbours, talking out
> of turn, 'burping in the classroom', passing wind, throwing
> rubbers, flicking 'gob' around on spoons, having book fights,
> making motor bike noises... (Tattum, 1982:90).

It has been observed that several things can be accomplished with successful

mucking about. For example,

> ... it could reveal how teachers would react under pressure, it
> could enhance the reputation of it instigator, it could flush out
> accomplices in the classroom and provide occasion for joint
> subversive action (Beynon and Atkinson, 1984:261).

In line with other British research that identified a considerable amount of

humour as students' "mucking around", Woods (1990:208-214) notes that "silly", "childish"

and "seemingly aimless behaviour" is an important dimension of school humour as students

transform "the reality of school from something they find tedious, irrelevant and perhaps

oppressive, to something more light-hearted and tolerable that they initiate and control." In

contrast to this type of humour which is seen as a combination of response to boredom and

the high spirits and energy level of students that meet with stifling aspects of schooling,

another type of laughter has been identified in the classroom. It is a laughter that is aimed at

reducing the power of the teacher. McLaren's (1986:160-161) analysis of rituals in a

Catholic school in Ontario refers to this as "laughter of resistance":

> The laughter of resistance is unlike any other. It occurs when
> the entire class -- or a significant number of students within the
> class -- spontaneously turns against the teacher. Usually the
> students wait patiently for an opening -- a 'slip-up' on the
> teacher's part (however slight) -- and, when the time is right,
> they begin to howl with laughter.

McLaren (1986:161) observed that laughter of resistance is different from other forms of laughter such as the communal laughter that follows the antics of a class clown, signifying the class' approval of the clown's actions. It is different from "laughter of merriment, which brings the body into a state of unalloyed euphoria" and "the laughter of the saint which fills the universe as it celebrates a sense of certainty." This type of laughter serves to mock and denounce. It is similar to that described by Woods (1990:214-222) as "subversive laughter", which can occur in situations where working class students find themselves in a middle class school, situations where authoritarian teachers are sensitive to challenges to their authority. The school culture developed by "the lads", as identified by Willis (1977) in his research on "how working class kids get working class jobs", shows the distinctive quality of the humour employed by the lads to resist school. As put by Woods (1990:220), this humour includes:

> ... playing with authority, devising practical jokes that mock teachers or conformists, 'ribbing' teachers, but ambiguously or anonymously, always just outside legitimate jurisdiction, indulging in a kind of 'marauding misbehaviour, throughout the school and especially on trips and among themselves,... and 'roughing each other up'.

On the surface it might often appear as if the sole purpose of student initiated humour in the classroom is that of pleasure. However, this review of the literature illustrates that it is more complex than plan fun. It may, for example, be significant in the development of self-images among the students, and in setting the parameters of teachers' identities in this setting.

28

Potential Dangers

Several dangers of classroom humour have been identified by Sudol (1981). While he argued that students do not learn well in classrooms run like prisons or boot camp, Sudol noted that telling funny stories or jokes, clowning around and teasing at the beginning of a class may set the wrong tone for the class. One of the dangers with telling funny stories or jokes at the beginning of a class, for example, is that some students may get the idea that the teacher is not going to get serious on that day so they join in with jokes to the extent that the classroom becomes too happy-go-lucky. Also, unless handled properly, punctuating lectures with anecdotes or comic ditties, which may be very useful in relieving the tedium, can be interpreted by some students as signalling the end of the formal lesson. A third danger with telling jokes in class is that these may be the only thing which certain students remember from the class.

Sudol (1981:27) reported that he played the clown in two different ways in the classroom: exaggerating and playing the fool. The former includes making a caricature of oneself, exaggerating one's features and mannerism. For instance, a teacher may grimace, shout or slam the blackboard to show his/her disagreement. In addition to inducing students think such a teacher is crazy, such actions can be deleterious to classroom control. Playing the fool for Sudol in the classroom includes pretending to know less than he actually does know. Some students may find such actions exasperating, even though they may get the point that the teacher does not want to be the source of answers. The idea of deliberately giving students wrong information in order to keep them on their toes runs the risk of students' not being able to see beneath the harlequin suit.

29

Other dangerous forms of classroom humour illustrated by Sudol include teasing and being sarcastic. He reported using teasing to develop closer relationships with his students, to show affection and concern for them. One such example of teasing was when he smilingly asked a boy, who was growing a beard, if he forgot to wash his face that day. In response the boy commented on the teacher's mustache. Such banter can lead to positive social relationships but it has its dangerous side as well, in that the teasing may be interpreting by the student to be insulting and offensive. Also, such teacher teasing may be seen as an indication that the teacher is one of the students, and consequently, the teacher may not get the respect he/she wanted.

Sarcasm, as a form of humour, is even more dangerous than teasing. While for many sarcasm has no place in teacher-student interaction, Sudol believed that sarcasm, if used without malice, can be a valuable teaching strategy. Here is his example:

> If say, Jennifer Adams has continually neglected to do her
> vocabulary homework, I may call on her repeatedly for
> definitions, even though I know full well that she hasn't done
> the work. When Jennifer replies with 'I didn't do it,' I will roll
> my eyes, shrug my shoulders, and with much ado say something
> to the effect of, 'Oh, that's right. I forgot. For the third week in
> a row Ms. Adams has decided it's better to remain locked in her
> dank, dark closet of ignorance while the rest of us bask in the
> warm sunlight of our new knowledge (Sudol, 1981: 28).

However, Sudol realized that the dangers of employing sarcasm are ever present because "if there is even the slightest tincture of meanness or malevolence in what" he says, "a student may become justifiably angered, offended, or alienated".

According to one writer (Hill, 1988:80-83) there are eleven things which teachers should avoid when they are using humour in the classroom. In summary form they are as follows: (1) Teachers should not make fun of students. Teachers and students may have different taste on things such as clothing and hair style and jokes around these tastes should be avoided; (2) Teachers should not explain the punch line of a joke, because it could be seen as insulting the intelligence of their students; (3) Teachers should not be negative when they are telling jokes. For example, they should not be "sarcastic, flippant or condescending", and they "should never humiliate, belittle or insult students, particularly in front of their peers;" (4) Teachers should feel the mood of the students before telling a joke. Do not inject a bit of humour because your lesson plan says so; humour is successful only when students are receptive to it; (5) Teachers should never make light of a serious situation. They must not convey that they do not care about their students. Important issues such as drugs, drinking, sex and grades must remain important and not the subject of jokes; (6) Teachers should avoid telling "currently popular jokes". Current television jokes circulating in the school may be successfully used later with a different punch line, but at the present time everyone, teachers and students, knows them; (7) Teachers must avoid "taboo language". The school is no place for dirty jokes and obscenities; (8) Teachers should not belittle their joke telling abilities, and should never evaluate a joke as "really funny" or "not that funny" before they tell it; (9) Teachers should never tell a joke without relating it to the lesson. Telling jokes for the sake of the joke is not acceptable to many students; (10) Teachers should avoid giving ambiguous messages in the jokes. This could mean that it may be necessary for teachers to explain what the joke teaches without explaining the joke as such; (11) Teachers' humour should never teach prejudice. There is no place for sexist, racist, or religious humour in the classroom.

Some of these points are also captured in Goodman's (1983:11) observations that it is important to distinguish between situations of "laughing with others" (i.e., constructive humour) and "laughing at others" (i.e., destructive humour). Here is his checklist for making this distinction.

Laughing with

1. going for the jocular vein
2. based on caring and empathy
3. builds confidence
4. involves people in the fun
5. a person makes a choice to be the butt of a joke (as in 'laughing at yourself')
6. amusing -- invites people to laugh
7. supportive
8. brings people closer
9. leads to positive repartee
10. pokes fun at universal human foibles

Laughing at

1. going for the jugular vein
2. based on contempt and insensitivity
3. destroys confidence through put downs
4. excludes some people
5. a person does not have a choice in being made the butt of a joke
6. abusing -- offends people
7. sarcastic
8. divides people
9. leads to one-downmanship cycle
10. reinforces stereotypes by singling out a particular group as the 'butt'

Before describing the theoretical orientation which guided the research on classroom humour reported in subsequent chapters of this book, it is appropriate to outline the focus of the research.

The Research Focus

A number of dimensions of school humour, including that associated with school administrators or seen to be part of the role of school counsellors, as well as humour in different parts of the school, have received varying amounts of attention from researchers and educators within the last three decades or so. Also, as is evident from the studies reported on in this chapter, different research methodologies have been employed in the quest to understand this facet of school life. Despite the long standing interest in school humour, it is obvious that there are still facets of it which have not been explored. By way of adding to our understanding of this part of school culture, the focus of the present research is on the student perspective on school humour. Some of the data analyzed here were collected as part of a larger study of the social construction of reality of schooling in Atlantic Canada. Other data were collected on specific examples of school humour, identified by observing the interactions in a number of classrooms with the aim of illustrating the presence of humour in this setting. Reviews of the core assumptions and concepts in the theoretical orientation which guided this research and details of the research process are presented in the following chapter.

CHAPTER 2

THEORETICAL ORIENTATION
AND RESEARCH PROCESS

The complexity of the biological, psychological and social processes associated with humour has challenged researchers and practitioners since the ancient Greeks proposed a theory of disease according to which a person's health was controlled by the balance of four humours (yellow bile, black bile, blood and phlegm). Aristotle and Plato gave credence to the view that laughter was the best medicine. The social history of humour includes Greek writings on buffoons and fools. More recently, a massive body of literature has developed on a multitude of topics related to humour in a wide range of arenas in society. For example, Nilsen's (1993) book on Humor Scholarship includes extensive bibliographies on humour in the media, fine arts, ethnicity, religion, science, mathematics, philosophy, gerontology and education. In addition, national styles of humour have received considerable attention over the years.

The purposes of this chapter are to highlight the core assumptions in the sociological orientation that provides the theoretical framework of the present study of school humour, to outline the data collection techniques followed here to research different aspects of such humour, and to describe how the qualitative data were analyzed. In these ways the chapter sets the stage for the presentation of our research findings and discussions of pedagogical and sociological issues relating to school humour.

Symbolic Interactionism

The term symbolic interactionism was first used by Blumer (1969) to designate what was then a relatively distinctive approach to the study of group life and human conduct. Over the years this approach has developed along with similar orientations (ethnomethodology, phenomenonology and constructivism) within an interpretative paradigm to have a major influence on sociological and educational research. For the purposes at hand, that is, the study of school humour, two of the overriding and interrelated issues within symbolic interactionism are worthy of note: meanings and identities. As revealed in students' comments relating to school humour and researchers' observations on classroom humour, meanings given to classroom situations and the identities of the participants therein are at the core of this dimension of school in general and classroom culture in particular.

Meanings

The three basic premises of symbolic interactionism regarding meanings are: (1) people act toward objects (things, symbols, other people, and even oneself) on the basis of the meanings that the objects have for them; (2) there is nothing inherent in an object which gives it its meaning(s), the meanings come from or arise out of the social interaction that people have with one another; and (3) the meanings are handled and modified through an interpretative process employed by people as they deal with the things they encounter.

These assumptions draw attention to the necessity of seeing human behaviour both in terms of external manifestations and internal processes. Classroom humour, for example, may be manifested through laughter or by less easily identifiable teacher and/or student actions and demeanour. Also, there is a subjective dimension to humour in that it is the meaning that a person gives to the action or event. It is the social construction of reality by individuals, so that not everyone in the setting may define something as funny. On the contrary, teachers and students are often noted to give different meanings to the same thing. In fact, an individual may change his/her mind and redefine the object giving it different meanings on separate occasions and consequently developing changing plans of action from one time to another.

The complexities of the dyadic relationship between subjectivism (including meanings and experiences) and objectivism (the world outside of the individual) continue to occupy researchers within the interpretative paradigm (see, for example, Jansen and Peshkin, 1992). Gidden (1986:537) uses the concept of "practical consciousness" to refer to the connection between the acting individual (subjective reality) and the institutions (objective reality) that are shaped and reshaped in the daily lives of individuals. While individuals give meanings to objects and the meanings may change over time, it is obvious that meanings get worked out within particular social contexts. Classroom humour may, to a large extent, be determined by the meanings which teachers and students have for each other's actions and interactions at any given time. Yet, those meanings arise within the institutional context of schooling.

The saliency of meanings to understanding humour is illustrated throughout the forthcoming chapters on school and classroom humour. At this point it is appropriate to elaborate on the process of identities, a sister concept to meanings.

Identities

Commencing with writings of Mead (1929; 1934), symbolic interactionists have developed a distinctive view of the "self". Briefly, the self is made up of two parts: "I" and "Me". The "I" is the active part of oneself, the initiator of actions. The "Me" is the passive part, it is constituted from the views of others. There is constant interaction between the "I" and the "Me". On the other hand, as noted by Hewitt and Hewitt (1986:130), these two parts of the self

> ... are phases of consciousness. At one moment in our conduct, we are alert to external stimuli and we respond to them. Almost immediately, we role-take, visualizing the direction of our conduct and the possible responses to it. In that moment our attention shifts to ourselves. 'I' and 'Me' ... are not tangible structures; they are only names for the two phases of self.

One's identity, that is, one's biographical sense of relationship to others, develops as the "I" and "Me" interact and are simultaneously present in the situation. Within the classroom, a student develops a sense of his or her identity relative to that of other students and teachers. Similarly, the identity of a teacher is influenced by his/her students. Both teachers and students may be anxious to portray particular types of identities so that others will be influenced to act in certain ways. The traditional authoritarian teacher and the notorious class clown are cases in point. Identities of students and teachers may be at stake as humour gets expressed in the classroom. Although it is difficult to pinpoint detailed features of those identities from the present research the significance of this concept is inductively illustrated with examples of students' comments and episodes of classroom humour.

37

The Research Process

The paradox of the traditional experimental approach to the study of humour is that the researcher decides what is humorous and then assumes that the subjects experience humour in the situation. Ethnographic research is based on the premise that what becomes defined as humour is subjective. Different students in the same classroom, for example, may have different meanings for the same actions, for the same episode of interaction. While some perceive it to be humorous others may not see it this way. In fact, as discussed in the above section on meanings, what a student perceives to be humorous on one occasion may not be seen as such by him/her at another time. Given this assumption, it is often difficult to uncover the subtle nuances of the humour at one time. However, it is believed that some aspects of humour in the natural setting can be identified through student comments on this dimension of school culture, comments given in response to an open ended question on a survey questionnaire. Other aspects of this facet of classroom culture can be illustrated through a combinations of observational and interview techniques. More specifically, in the present study observations of laughter, smiles, giggles and other actions that were seen to be suggestive of someone perceiving something to be humorous were followed by interviews with the participants in the situation.

Questionnaire

As part of a larger study of the schooling experiences of high school students in Atlantic Canada, a survey questionnaire was administered by either the researcher or a research assistant to 20,351 high school students. Those students represented schools selected by means of random sample, stratified according to district, school board, school

38

size, community size, religion (Newfoundland and Labrador), language (New Brunswick),

and type of school (e.g., senior high, junior-senior high, or all-grade).

The data base for the presentation on student views on school humour, Part II

of this book, consists of student responses to the last item on that questionnaire. The item

was phrased as follows:

> Obviously this questionnaire covers only a small part of your
> experiences in the school. Please outline other aspects of your
> experiences in the school which concern you. Fell free to add
> any views you might have concerning your school, your
> teachers, your textbooks, and the way you are expected to
> study.

Table 1 provides a statistical breakdown by province of the number of students

surveyed, the number of students choosing to respond to the last item on the questionnaire,

and the number of students making observations related to school humour.

TABLE 2-1

**STUDENTS RESPONDING TO REQUEST TO OUTLINE ASPECTS OF
SCHOOLING EXPERIENCE OF CONCERN TO THEM**

Province	Students Surveyed	Responding to Request	Commenting on School Humor
New Brunswick	5,534	5,054	282
Newfoundland	7,987	6,065	360
Nova Scotia	5,202	4,271	231
Prince Edward Island	1,637	1,374	76
TOTALS	20,351	16,764	879

The topics covered by the questionnaire items were highly varied and included

such matters as student councils, school prefects, school rules, disciplinary procedures,

39

participation in extra-curricular activities, teacher cooperation, and student attitudes toward school. Even though the questionnaire makes no reference to humour as such, some of the items may have helped simulate students to reflect upon certain dimensions of humour, or the lack thereof, in the school. For example, one question read:

> Sometimes students approach teachers individually to talk to them about certain things, while at other times students like to be in groups of two or more as they talk to teachers about different things. How often do students in your classroom do the following individually and in groups? Indicate what you think is the appropriate frequency for each type of approach concerning each of the following by placing check mark in the appropriate space.

One item in this question focused on the amount of freedom given to individuals and groups in the classroom and school. Other items asked students to indicate the frequency with which students were given the freedom they desire or with which they were given too much freedom.

Students were also asked to agree or disagree with a number of statements including the following: I usually enjoy school, school is a waste of time; you can't run a school unless the students behave themselves; having good friends is one of the most important things to me in school; I want my teachers to like me; and I find school exciting.

The richness of students' comments on school humour as given in response to last question of the questionnaire went far beyond any dimension of humour in teacher-student and/or student-student interactions tapped by the preceding items, which no doubt provides evidence of the salience for students of that aspects of their schooling experiences.

Classroom Observations

The observational phase of this research falls into two distinct parts. During the first part observational studies were conducted in nine schools: four in Newfoundland and Labrador, two in Nova Scotia, two in New Brunswick (one English and one French), and one in Prince Edward Island. These schools included two all-grade schools, two with elementary through high school grades and five with junior and senior high students. Each school was studied as a distinct case where the researcher attempted to explore different dimensions of the schooling experiences of students. A researcher spent from four to eight consecutive weeks in each of these nine schools. These case studies were conducted over a five year period. In addition to researching the written documents relating to the school organization and curriculum, the researcher was a nonparticipant observer in the school. Students were observed in all parts of the school: corridors, cafeteria, gymnasium and classrooms. Observations were made on, and students were interviewed about, a range of matters including academic performance and evaluation, curriculum and textbooks, extracurricular activities, homework, methods of discipline, school rules, student aspirations, student-teacher and student-student relationships in the school. The present book was developed from the observations on only one issue that came to the fore during classroom observations: classroom humour.

For the classroom observations, the researcher sat at the back of the classroom, usually in a corner. As many notes as possible were taken on everything observed that seemed to be humorous -- or intended to be humorous -- by student or teacher. As soon as possible after observations, students and teachers who were seen to be the key

41

participants in the humour were interviewed, usually in an informal manner. In fact, many of the interviews may be more aptly described as informal conversations that took place in the classroom, in the corridors and other places where the opportunity arose to get participants' views on the interaction episodes recorded as humorous by the researcher. While these conversations followed no formal pattern, the researcher had pre set questions to help identify what the participants saw as humorous and their reasons for perceiving those situations as such.

The second part of the observational phase of this study came after the intensive and broadly based research into these nine schools had been completed. This part was not designed as a research project unto itself, that is, with a particular time frame and a selected number of schools and classrooms, as was the case in the first part of the observational phase. The intent was to observe classrooms whenever the opportunity arose, with the aim of recording examples of classroom humour. Over a period of four years the researcher observed in six classrooms in as many high schools for times ranging from three to seven class periods. Notes were taken on each episode of humour observed and conversations were held with the key players as soon as possible after the observations were made.

As described above for both the first and second parts of the observational phases of this research, observing and interviewing may appear to be straightforward and clear cut. However, several problems were experienced in the present research which should be noted here. First,anyone looking for a precise definition of humour will probably be disappointed to find that it includes a wide range of social processes and a large number of interaction strategies. It has been observed that "humour is a slippery subject" whose

"nature and mechanisms are notoriously difficult to analyze" (Goodson and Walker,

1991:29). One relatively simple definition of humour is the "warmhearted, sympathetic, or

good-natured treatment of small failings or ironies, those that prompt similes rather than

laughter or derision" (Hayakawa, 1987: 285). While they refer to other aspects of social

interaction within a broader framework of humour, Hayakawa offers the following words as

synonyms of humorous: comic, comical, droll, facetious, funny, jocose, jocular, waggish and

witty. Something is said to be humorous when it causes amusement or laughter. As obvious

as this statement may appear, the complexities associated with identifying the humorous in

this way are quickly realized when one observes the characteristics of laughter in different

situations. The variation that may exist from giggles and titters, to snickers and sniggers, to

chuckles and chortles, to loud, hearty and spontaneous roars is testimony to the complex

social processes of humour and the situational structures that provide the parameters of these

processes. The difficulty in identifying and analyzing humour is in part due to the fact it is

not a static quality that is built into an event, a statement, or a story. Rather, it is built, for

instance, on misunderstandings or inappropriate usage of words, and is reflected in a flow of

energy that is difficult to predict. For example, Goodson and Walker (1991:29) noted some

differences between jokes and the comic. Accordingly, they observed that jokes are humour

that survives reduction to script, are products of formal situations, demand an audience, are

told at a particular time, and have a start and an end. On the other hand, comic is humour

that arises from the tension and ambiguity in the situation, humour brought on by the comic relationship that develops in the situation, offers identity through sharing of meanings, is seamless and irrepressible, and thrives between equals in the face of authority.

A second problem experienced in the present classroom observations is associated with the multitude of classroom happenings during any one forty-five minute class period. It was often difficult, and sometimes impossible, to see everything that was happening at any one time.

Thirdly, it is usually difficult to record everything that one observes even when the observations are confined to what may be seen as humorous by one person or another in this setting.

Fourthly, the ideal of talking with, and probing into the inner meanings of, each of the key players in the observed humour in an attempt to understand how each experienced the situation in question is rarely achieved. The work of the classroom and school goes on as the researcher, who is an outsider, attempts to become an insider in terms of the experiences of the students and teachers in specific events isolated by the researcher.

Finally, dealing specifically with the issue of classroom humour, the strategy of pinpointing specific episodes of interaction with somewhat clearly defined boundaries, that is as having a beginning and an ending, can be misleading. It is likely that much classroom humour is connected in some ways to previous events, meanings and identities in the classroom. It is realized that this continuity is not revealed by looking at episodes in isolation. However, those episodes can be revealing with respect to the social context of classroom humour and the forms in which it is expressed.

Data Analysis

In line with the data collection strategies this book is written from three types of qualitative data: (1) students written responses to a request for them to comment on whatever aspect of their schooling experiences they so choose; (2) records made from classroom observations of humour in this setting; and (3) notes taken on interviews with students and teachers. Notes taken on each episode of humour during classroom observations were combined with those gathered from interviews and conversations relating to the same episode to develop as complete a description as possible, and to facilitate a greater understanding of the causes and consequences, of such episodes of classroom humour. To elaborate on the processes of data analysis, it is necessary to focus separately on analyzing student responses to the open ended question and the procedure followed in analyzing classroom observations.

Analyzing Student Responses

Student responses to a request for them to comment on any aspects of their schooling experiences which concern them were examined to identify any general themes they might exhibit. A theme was identified as such when a degree of theoretical saturation was reached, that is, when no additional data were found whereby the researchers could develop properties of the category (Glaser and Strauss, 1967; Glaser, 1978; 1982). In other words, in order to be identified as a theme the topic or issue had to be found to be recurring in the comments of students from different schools. Among the general themes identified and reported on elsewhere are teachers' pets and class victims (Martin, 1982; 1985c); helpful, understanding and co-operative teachers (Martin, 1983; 1985c); student embarrassment (Martin, 1985b; 1985c); school rules (Martin and Baksh, 1984; Martin 1985c); homework (Martin, 1985c); teacher expectation (Baksh and Martin, 1983) and teaching strategies (Baksh and Martin, 1986). In the present analysis, comments relating to school humour were studied further in an attempt to identify themes within this general area of concern among high school students in Atlantic Canada. The major themes identified as implicit in the students' responses relating to school humour include those linked to the school climate, joking in the classroom, teacher characteristics and in-group processes and the social-emotional dimensions of classroom humour. Each of these four themes became the subject of a chapter, for a total of four chapters in Part II of this book. Comments pertaining to each are further analyzed for the purpose of delineating more specific topics within it and such sub-topics constitute the subheadings within the chapters. It is important to note that, while the themes are discussed individually, they are often interrelated in the day-to-day interactions in the school. For example, the issue of school climate is obviously an integral part of the social-emotional dimensions of classroom life. Similarly, joking in the classroom is linked to individual characteristics and group processes. In the interest of clarity and presentational convenience, however, the themes and their sub-topics are in general treated separately. Taken together, they comprise a diversity of meanings and interpretations which offer testimony regarding the complexity of factors relating to the way students experience humour in the classroom and to the playing out of student and teacher identities in this setting.

Analyzing Observational Data

As described above in the observational and interview phase of data collection, episodes of classroom humour were recorded in varying details during, and immediately after, the observations were made and interviews were conducted with the primary participants. While different ways of analyzing and presenting those episodes were entertained at points along the way in the research process, it was not until the observations had been completed and the episodes of classroom humour were reviewed in total that the idea of focusing on the context and forms of classroom humour emerged. Hence, the focus on the context of classroom humour as presented here, that is, as including the institutional, organizational and curriculum environments, evolved from a study of the classroom observations recorded during the observational phase of this research. The sociological orientation of this research underlines the significance of teacher and student identities in day-to-day interactions in the classroom. However, the idea of viewing those identities as part of the social context of classroom humour was formulated as we studied different episodes of classroom humour recorded in this research.

Even though there was an awareness of the variety and significance of forms of classroom humour early in the observational phase of this research, the decision to focus on the forms of classroom humour as a topic in itself came later in the research process.

The strategy of presenting episodes of humour as a means of illustrating different dimensions of the context of classroom humour and as a way of showing the different forms of humour in this setting was adopted for other reasons as well. One argument is that by letting different situations of classroom humour speak for themselves, to

47

whatever extent this is possible from our descriptions of the interactions and classroom setting, the reader is drawn closer to the experiences of teachers and students than would be the case if they were not included in this manner. Also, given the nature of classroom humour as reflected in those episodes, the reader may want to study them for other interpretations and, thereby, gain greater insights into the culture of classroom humour.

By way of combining students' views on classroom humour with the context and forms of this humour as suggested through classroom observations, the final chapter in this book attempts to take the analysis beyond the substantive issues to another level, that of developing a grounded theory of classroom humour.

PART II

STUDENT VIEWS ON SCHOOL HUMOUR IN ATLANTIC CANADA

This part of the book presents an analysis of comments collected from 879 high school students in Atlantic Canada relating to school humour. First, their comments were placed into four groupings according to their overall themes, which are identified here as school climate (Chapter 3), joking in the classroom (Chapter 4), individual characteristics and group processes (Chapter 5), and social-emotional dimensions of classroom humour. Second, the comments in each of these themes were further divided into different groupings and sub-groupings. Within the school climate themes are those dealing with (1) sources and characteristics of a fun atmosphere in the school, (2) social distance and (3) school spirit. Issues about joking in the classroom are identified as: (1) reciprocity in joking relationships, (2) benefits of classroom humour, (3) negative consequences of humour, and (4) the use of stupid jokes. Among the individual characteristics and group processes noted in students' comments on school humour are: (1) characteristics of good teachers, (2) age of teacher, (3) student maturity, (4) teacher's gender, and (5) the presence of in-groups. The social-emotional dimensions of school life, as seen in comments from high school students participating in this part of the present study, revolve around (1) the differential treatment along the lines of pets-victims phenomena, (2) sarcastic remarks from teachers, (3) the process of making fun of students, and (3) teachers' moods.

CHAPTER 3

SCHOOL CLIMATE

The idea of "school climate" has received considerable attention over the years from researchers and practitioners alike. At different times it has been referred to as the atmosphere, the tone, or the personality of the school. School climates, as they have been described, vary on a continuum ranging from warm to cold (sometimes referred to as open versus closed climates). Analyses of school climates have included a focus on personal aspects of individuals (for example, consideration for one another as opposed to aloofness) and the organizational demands (for example, esprit de corps versus expectations that hinder informal relationships) on them. Without always referring to the presence or absence of humour in teacher-student relationships or among the students themselves, students from different schools in each of the four Atlantic provinces offered comments that suggested the types of school climate that seemed to be most conducive to the development of positive school humour. Their comments can be placed in one of three overlapping categories outlined here as fun atmosphere, social distance, and school spirit.

A Fun Atmosphere

Students from each of the four Atlantic provinces identified a number of aspects relating to the "fun atmosphere" of schooling, including (1) the contrast between having "fun" and being "bored" in school, (2) the need for fun in school, (3) friends as a prerequisite for fun, (4) teachers as creators of a fun atmosphere, (5) fun and learning, (6) fun outside the classroom.

51

Fun versus Boredom

It is not surprising that different students contrasted the fun and boring dimensions

of schooling:

> ...school is exciting sometimes, but is often a little boring here....
> (Grade 11 girl, Prince Edward Island)

> I like school most of the time but when you do things over and
> over again it's boring. It's fun to learn new things and to get
> ahead in the world but if you don't try you'll never get to the top.
> (Grade 9 girl, Prince Edward Island)

> School can be lots of fun but sometimes it can be a real drag.
> (Grad 9 girl, Prince Edward Island)

> School is generally fun. A few classes are boring but I can say so
> far that its been fun.
> (Grade 9 girl, New Brunswick)

> I have found that school can be fun and learning can be fun and
> not boring if you do things certain ways.
> (Grade 10 boy, New Brunswick)

A Grade 9 Nova Scotia girl observed: "If you can't have fun in school, it is going

to be boring all the time." According to a Grade 12 boy in Prince Edward Island, "if school

was not boring and more fun students would not break the rules". On the other hand, a New

Brunswick Grade 12 girl observed: "A school is only what you make it to be." She added: "It

can be fun if you make it fun."

Need for Fun

The student perceived need for "fun" was suggested by the Grade 9 boy in

Newfoundland and Labrador who claimed that "if the students did have more fun" they "would

enjoy school much more and things will be much better." Similarly, a Grade 10 girl in New

Brunswick expressed the need for "more fun ... in school" which would "bring more excitement

to the school". A New Brunswick boy commented that he went "to school to learn and have fun
at the same time". While he reported liking "the occasional practical joke" he drew the "line
at vandalism". As seen in different comments, the need for fun is associated with need
relaxation:

> I think that school should be a lot more relaxed, and not half as
> much pressure as the students have on them now, it is quite
> difficult to do this, but I think an effort should be made not only
> to make it relaxed and exciting, but fun too.
> (Grade 9 boy, Prince Edward Island)

> I would like to see more classes with a relaxed atmosphere, which
> is more fun and helps people to learn easier. If this relaxed
> atmosphere is obtained, the student feels free to voice his or her
> opinions and this makes it easier to learn.
> (Grade 9 boy, Nova Scotia)

The importance of a fun atmosphere was noted by one Grade 12 boy in Nova
Scotia in his report of the change that took place in his school, and how this change affected his
attitude toward schooling:

> School should be enjoyed, and students should not have to worry
> about being kicked out for everything wrong they do. Also if a
> student is not doing well he should be encouraged not locked up
> in a room with books put in front of him and told 'study or you're
> out!' They should encourage you to see teachers. But here they
> don't. This used to be a nice place to come to at one time. You
> actually liked school and all the fun that went along with it but
> now for one I don't any more.

Another Nova Scotia student, a Grade 12 girl, alluded to the positive aspects of
a fun atmosphere when she complained about the changing nature of the atmosphere in her
school:

> School should be enjoyable but, at least for me, it is starting to
> become a dislike chore. We should feel comfortable here but now
> it is starting to become an impersonal function in which we are

treated, usually not always, as one person of a group. Personal
contact seems to be dwindling greatly. A poor simulation is a
heard of 1000 sheep, if one is lost, don't worry, we still have the
other 999, one lost won't hurt us. Just forget about them. That
attitude is becoming too dominant and is lessening the feeling of
good we should have about our school and the education we
receive. The fun atmosphere is dwindling.

However, as noted by a Grade 10 girl in yet another Nova Scotia school, students

"can't be turned off just because you find one part of the subject... or a part of the year bad."

Student perceived benefit of a fun atmosphere for the teachers was indicated by

a Grade 10 boy in Nova Scotia who wrote:

Teachers should have a good time during class. This makes it fun
for everybody even the teachers will be more relaxed and feel
better about his or her work.

Friends: a Prerequisite for Fun

Students have noted the necessity of having friendships among themselves and of

being friends with teachers in the development of a fun atmosphere in the school. At this point,

it is sufficient to illustrate students' views on the association between fun and having friends,

a theme which is developed below. Examples of their comments on the presence of in-group

joking relationships in the school are presented in Chapter 6.

Peers as Friends

It is common knowledge that friends play major roles in the self and related

socialization processes of the world of young adults. A fairly wide of sample of students in the

present research noted that having friends within one's peer group is an important aspect of

school life. Focusing specifically on the association between having friends and the fun

dimension of schooling, a Grade 12 student in New Brunswick wrote: "Your friends really make school for you." He added that "school, particularly high school, are some of the best and most fun and enjoyable years of" one's "whole life". One Grade 9 girl in Nova Scotia reported that "school is fun" and she enjoys "it very much because" she had "good friends" in there whom she likes "to be with". A second Nova Scotia girl (Grade 10) claimed that her main reason for coming to school is "to see" her "friends and be with them and laugh with them". Yet another Grade 10 girl commented that she did not "enjoy school, but she liked "all the fun" of "being with" her "friends there".

Different students made reference to their love for learning while commenting on the importance of friends in creating a fun atmosphere in the school.

> I enjoy school very much because I love to learn and I have many friends.
> (Grade 9 girl, Nova Scotia)

> ...my general opinion is that school is fun due to friends and the joy of learning.
> (Grade 12 boy, Nova Scotia)

> I enjoy school, not because it is a learning experience although that has something to do with it. I enjoy being around lots of people and friends and having fun. I usually have a good time at school along with getting good grades.
> (Grade 12 girl, Nova Scotia)

> I really enjoy school and it helps me get a good outlook on life. When I think of school I think of learning, a place where I can get my education and also a place where I can socialize and find new friends.
> (Grade 10 girl, New Brunswick)

> I think school is fun in a way. You can see your friends and learn the facts of life.
> (Grade 9 girl, New Brunswick)

It makes you feel better to know that you can make friends, be responsible, be trustful, make people want to be like you and make them better as an individual.
(Grade 11 girl, Prince Edward Island)

I found school... gave students a time to be with old friends and to make new friends. It also was a time to begin relationships with others. This is one thing which makes the school life more exciting and enjoyable.
(Grade 12 boy, Prince Edward Island)

Teachers as Friends

An earlier publication has highlighted the student perceived significance of having "friendly teachers" for teacher-student relationships in general and for teaching and learning in particular (Martin, 1983:47-77). In the present focus on the fun atmosphere as providing a context for school humour, it is appropriate to give examples of students' observations as they address the need for teachers to be friends of the students, the potentially positive results of such a teacher-student relationship, and the parameters that must be respected in such relationships if teachers are to be successful in maintaining social order.

Here is a sample of students' views on the desirability of having teachers as their friends:

Teachers should not act superior in any way to students, this often causes dislike for the teacher. They should try to be friends rather than superiors.
(Grade 11 girl, Nova Scotia)

I believe teachers should bring themselves down to our level.
(Grade 11 girl, Newfoundland and Labrador)

Teachers should consider a student, not only as a student but a friend.
(Grade 11 girl, Newfoundland and Labrador)

56

Teachers and staff should try to be more of a friend to the student rather than a parent.
(Grade 9 girl, Newfoundland and Labrador)

I feel a good teacher is one who teaches the subject they are supposed to be teaching plus be friendly and add a few jokes.
(Grade 10 girl, Nova Scotia)

Teachers should make better attempts to be more friendly instead of so damn impersonal and aloof.
(Grade 12, girl, Nova Scotia)

A Nova Scotia boy in Grade 10 observed that teachers should make a special effort to be friends with "shy students". And a Grade 10 girl in Newfoundland and Labrador reported that her teacher's have changed "for the better" in that "they now treat" the students "as friend" and "joke with" them.

Some of the student-perceived results of having friendly teachers are identified in the following quotations:

If students and teachers were more like friends and had a friendly relationship there would be allot more accomplished.
(Grade 12 boy, Prince Edward Island)

....the teachers are helpful -- many of them seem more as a friend than a teacher.
(Grade 12 girl, New Brunswick)

I also feel that teachers should be more friendly so that when you want help you do not feel like an idiot.
(Grade 11 boy, New Brunswick)

I think the students should be able to relate to the teachers like a friend and maybe students can work better or feel more at ease in school.
(Grade 10 girl, New Brunswick)

A small number of students went so far as to suggest that they should be on a first name basis with their teachers. In the words of Grade 12 girl in Nova Scotia,

57

> I feel school would be a better place if the teachers would come down to the students' level in Senior High, making students feel more equal with them.... By being on a first name basis, students would feel more relaxed around teachers in the school.

On the other hand, many students noted that there are certain limits to the extent to which teachers should be friendly with their students. In the view of a Grade 12 boy in Nova Scotia, "Teachers should be teachers first and buddy's second not vice versa." After observing that her "teachers... are mostly friendly and you know you can joke with them", a Grade 12 girl in Prince Edward Island added: "but you know when to be serious too". While arguing that teachers "should be friendly", a Nova Scotia Grade 12 boy pointed out that they "should be able to keep the class in control". Similarly, Grade 10 girl in another school in that province opined that while teachers "should be friendly" they "shouldn't get too friendly".

In reference to teachers as friends, some students noted that the friendship dimension of student-teacher relationship was most evident outside of the classroom, and even away from the school environment altogether. The observation that teacher-student relationships in the classroom are different from their relationships in other settings is suggestive of a distinction between humour in the classroom and that employed by teachers and students as they interact with each another in other places.

Teachers: Initiators of a Fun Atmosphere

While it is clear that students' attitudes and actions are important in the development of a fun atmosphere in the school, students from different provinces identified the teacher as the initiator of this type of a classroom atmosphere. Students have suggested that the extent to which teachers create a fun atmosphere in the classroom is associated with a number of variables including how well a teacher knows his/her subject, as is evident when a Grade 9 boy in Nova Scotia claimed that "teachers who don't know what they are talking about are as boring as hell". The need for teachers who are genuinely interested in their subjects as well as in the students was also noted by different students to be associated with teachers' predisposition toward a fun classroom atmosphere. The following comments where made in the context of observations on teachers who "are fun to be with" or "don't mind a little fun":

> Teachers should be interested in the subjects not just teach the books.
> (Grade 11 boy, Newfoundland and Labrador)
>
> How can he teach us if he is not interested in what we are doing? He does not know how our feelings.
> (Grade 12 girl, Prince Edward Island)
>
> Our teachers lack enthusiasm, although I respect my teachers I feel many of them have little drive or stamina. If the teachers enjoyed what they taught or showed enthusiasm, students would begin to wake up.
> (Grade 11 girl, New Brunswick)

In addition, teachers need to have a desire to make school fun for their students. For example, one Grade 10 girl in New Brunswick complained:

> I find that our teachers for the most part have very little interest in making school fun. They over emphasize exams and only teach us what is completely necessary. This makes for a very boring school life.

Here are additional illustrations of other comments that suggest the need for teachers to put more fun in the teaching-learning endeavour:

> From my experience in school I feel that the teachers need to retain the students attention more than teaching a lesson. The teachers need to put fun in the act of learning.
> (Grade 12 girl, Nova Scotia)

59

School is fun, but I feel teachers should take more time to explain things, and try to make school more than just a place to work and study.
(Grade 9 girl, New Brunswick)

School can be fun when high people do not go to extremes with their ideas for us students.
(Grade 12 girl, New Brunswick - translated French)

I find that some of our teachers do not put fun into learning, I think that this is one of the reasons for students being noisy. I think that teachers should make learning fun the students as well as for themselves.
(Grade 9 girl, Newfoundland and Labrador)

A Grade 11 girl in Nova Scotia mirrored the observations of others in her observation: "The teachers and the classroom atmosphere are important if a student is going to be interested in the subject being taught." She added that a teacher "should have a fun, interesting class", otherwise, students "will not work" to the extend required to "do good in school".

It has been observed that teachers can make a subject "interesting and "fun". To quote a Grade 12 boy in New Brunswick,

In the run of a day at this school the only class I really learn anything that is not only interesting, but fun, is Geography. Mr. ... makes it fun to learn in his class.

After reporting on that Biology was "hard" and "boring" in the previous year, a Grade 11 New Brunswick student girl wrote: "Now Biology is fun, but the tests are too hard." While complaining about the amount of reading expected in the Literature course, a Grade 11 boy in Newfoundland had praise for his teacher who "made it interesting" and motivated students "to learn something" in his class. In contrast, a Grade 12 girl in Nova Scotia opined:

> In English I think as it is an essential course, it should not be so
> boring. The teacher should be relaxed and not so serious. An
> occasional joke is needed.

A similar complaint about the teaching of French came from a Grade 10 boy in Nova Scotia who

wrote:

> I have found that school can be fun and learning can be fun and
> not boring if you do things certain ways. The way they teach
> French is very boring and it should be taught more actively and
> allow students to participate.

Given the positive attitudes students have toward teachers whom they see as

promoting a fun atmosphere in the classroom, it not surprising that some of them reported doing

"better" in subjects that are taught by "fun teachers" than they do in those taught by teachers

who are not fun to be with. For example, a Grade 9 boy in Nova Scotia wrote that he passes,

"with flying colors", the subjects taught by "teachers that are fun to be with".

Fun and Learning

The observations of students who commented on "fun" and "learning"

simultaneously include the following views: students can "have fun while .. learning"; fun and

learning are separate, but necessary, processes in the school; "school can be fun if you want it

to be fun"; students can have fun in school "even though most rules say you cannot"; most of

the student "fun is not intended to cause trouble for our teachers"; while "the attitude... if you

do good in school you can't have fun" is found among some teachers and students it is not a

widely held view; "school can be boring and it can be fun"; and when school is no longer fun,

some students "will stop going."

Fun Outside of the Classroom

In addition to the desirability of creating a fun atmosphere in the classroom, thereby making teaching-learning processes more interesting, the fun aspects of schooling outside of the classroom have also been commented upon by students. One of those aspects is the student view that teachers should be fun to be with outside the classroom. To quote three students,

> I am friendly with all my teachers and some of them I consider my friends. .... The teachers who are friendly outside of class, and command respect, attention, etc. during class and in the school are the classes in which I get a lot of work completed.
> (Grade 10 girl, Nova Scotia)

> I have seen how working together outside of class time can be a fun and learning experience for the students involved. It gives them a chance to learn more about their fellow students and how to cooperate and work with them and get along better with them. This creates a less formal atmosphere in the class which, I feel, is the best atmosphere to learn in.
> (Grade 11 girl, New Brunswick)

> Teachers who talk to you in school are fun to be with. It is a pleasure to be around them.
> (Grade 11 boy, Newfoundland and Labrador)

Another aspect of the fun atmosphere in the school, but outside of the classroom, is in the students' view the need for extracurricular activities:

> We should have more school dances and fun things that everyone likes and not just some of the people like.
> (Grade 12 girl, Prince Edward Island)

> There should be more fun in school, something should be held once a week (during school time) to break the boredom and to give students something to look forward to....
> (Grade 11 boy, New Brunswick)

I think our school should have more activities to get more students
involved and improve school spirit.
Grade 12 girl, New Brunswick)

There should be more fun aspects i.e, sports in school.
(Grade 9 girl, Nova Scotia)

Social Distance

Intertwined with the extent to which teachers and students are friends is the issue

of what may be referred to as social distance in the classroom. More specifically, the question

is: Do students see teachers as being aloof or as sharing an informal relationship with them in

the classroom? The student view that teachers often maintain a social distance from their

students is illustrated by a Grade 12 girl in Nova Scotia who, after observing that teachers are

not "on the students' level", wrote:

> I think teachers should make an effort to be friends as well as
> teachers to their students. ... They should, as students get older
> and more mature, try to be on the same level as the students, not
> just on a teacher level, as an older wiser person.

Similarly, a Grade 12 boy in New Brunswick thought that "the older more experienced" teachers

tend to maintain a greater social distance from students than the younger ones do:

> Most of the teachers (usually the older more experienced ones)
> treat everyone like inferiors and seem to just putting in time....
> The younger teachers are usually much more friendly.

This student went on to suggest that if teachers were closer to their students the students would

learn more:

> I feel that if a teacher can treat a student as a friend and not be set
> in his ways teaching that I can learn allot more.

She continued her argument by pointing to the need for teachers "to be able to joke around" and

thereby reduce the social distance between teacher and student:

63

There is no reason that teachers shouldn't be able to joke around
with students, it seems it would help to clear the air and make
sitting in a stuffy classroom a little better.

A Grade 12 girl in New Brunswick expressed the thought that teachers, as

revealed by their unwillingness to admit to their mistakes, often want to appear to be superior.

Teachers should be more willing to admit they are human, they
can make mistakes, and that our opinion of them won't lessen
because we realize they are human.

Another New Brunswick girl (Grade 10) in different school complained:

... most teachers think they can stand up there and look down at
us in our seats, they are God!

Other student comments can be used to further illustrate their views on teachers

and administrators whom they perceive to be distant from their students:

Most teachers are willing to give extra help if required, but usually
imply it to be a vast imposition on their time. Many have a great
status problem and try to make students feel inferior to them.
(Grade 12 girl, New Brunswick)

Some teachers don't take the time to talk to you one-to-one to see
why you are the way you are. Some teachers are too distant so
therefore, they can't communicate with you and understand you.
(Grade 12 girl, New Brunswick)

I enjoy coming to school because it gives me some thing to do and
I like some of the people here. I feel that students and teachers
would get along better if the teachers would treat students as
people and not just part of a job. I get along really well with my
teachers who talk on my level (i.e., a human being) then as if I
was just another kid to drill homework into. I find this not only
with teachers but most adults. Our principal is the best principal
in the world. He talks to us....
(Grade 12 boy,New Brunswick)

I think that the relationship between the students and the teachers
would become better if the teachers didn't act bossy, but like a
friend. My opinion of some teachers is that they act too bossy

64

almost worse than parents do in some ways. The teacher should
act like human beings.
(Grade 9 girl, Nova Scotia)

... teachers are often condensing, obnoxious, others are pleasant.
(Grade 12 boy, Nova Scotia)

I wish to note that some of the teachers and the principals should
show some good manners toward the students instead of being
stuck-up.
(Grade 12 girl, Nova Scotia)

School size may be an important variable in the social distance that exist between

teachers and students in the school. For example, a Grade 10 girl in Nova Scotia wrote:

I used to attend a larger school and I find this school is a little
more casual. This is good because I feel that the students and
teachers are able to communicate better; it promotes a better
relationship between teachers and students.

On the other hand, different teachers within the same school may be seen to be promoting

different types of relationships with their students:

One teacher -- Mr. ... was not my favourite teacher. He made
you feel really stupid if you didn't answer a question right. But
this is only one teacher. My favoured teacher (even though I
didn't have him for any subjects) is Mr. .... Now he's pretty
cool. He's just like one of the kids.
(Grade 12 girl, Nova Scotia)

At different points in this review of students' observations relating to school

humour, comments are presented which suggest that students sometimes see teachers as

maintaining a considerable social distance from them (See, for example, the section on "student

maturity" in Chapter 5). Conversely, certain teachers are seen to be friendly, as noted above,

and willing to participate in joking relations with their students , and to inject humour in teacher-

65

learning processes (See, for example, "humorous versus serious teachers" and "benefits of classroom humour" in Chapter 4).

School Spirit

Each of the foregoing issues presented under the headings "fun atmosphere" and "social distance" may be viewed as intricately intertwined with school spirit. However, since students often commented on school spirit without referring to either of these topics it is appropriate to deal with that phenomenon as a separate topic at this time. Without giving details of the widespread concern among students over the lack of school spirit in their respective schools, on the one hand, and the positive results of a healthy school spirit in other schools, on the other hand, the present focus on school spirit is designed to indicate the significance of particular aspects of school climate for the development of school humour. In fact, the extent and nature of school humour present in a school may be regarded as an indicator of the nature of the school climate. By way of addressing the issue at hand, it is appropriate to note the contrasting types of relationships in different schools and to illustrate potential impact of school size on school spirit.

Contrasting Relationships

One of the more striking things about students observations on school spirit is the contrasting nature of the relationships between teachers and students in schools with a good school spirit and those without such a sense of informality, involvement and identity. According to different students the absence of a school spirit has a negative impact on teacher-student relationships in general and on the joking relationships in particular:

66

I find in this school there is no school spirit. People seem to come just to be here and it's boring. You can't laugh ... can't talk to anyone.
(Grade 11 girl Nova Scotia)

I believe that our schooling is lacking school spirit and the student council should try to involve students in activities rather than just the everyday classes. ... We need to talk and joke with teachers.
(Grade 9 boy, Nova Scotia)

In contrast, other students representing each of the four provinces in Atlantic Canada reported that their schools reaped the benefits of well developed school spirits:

I feel that this school ... is a very close knit school. Most people here give me a very good impression of school and therefore I enjoy school. The activities are what really bring the 3 areas together.
(Grade 11 girl, New Brunswick)

Another good thing about this school is the school spirit we have. Most people try to get out to see the sports activities. Another thing is that you know everyone and that makes it a lot easier to go to school even if it is just to see your friends.
(Grade 10 girl, New Brunswick)

Schools have fun activities in which I enjoy. Sports are fun and our school has allot going for it and the teachers are exceptionally well. It's a great school spirit.
(Grade 10 girl, Nova Scotia)

Some of the teachers are nice. They joke around a bit but does not carry it too far. We have a good school spirit which is good because students need a little bit of fun to make a subject more interesting.
(Grade 9 girl, Newfoundland and Labrador)

Students as well as teachers may be the culprits in the lack of a generally desirable school spirit. To quote a Grade 12 girl in New Brunswick,

The atmosphere of this school is full of spirit and friendliness. Support is given when needed, not just from students but from teachers as well. However, many students can be very mean and cruel to other students as well as to teachers. These students in particular think they are hot shots and usually don't get their just punishment and can ruin, and usually do, a student's year at High School.

Similarly, another New Brunswick Grade 12 student, a girl in a second school wrote:

We at... are very fortunate we have tremendous school spirit, and our principal gives us a lot of freedom, but many people abuse this. They have no respect for him or the school.

Student Groups

While the presence of student groups (formal and informal groups) can add to a school's spirit, the school spirit may suffer on occasion because of group rivalry. To illustrate with the comments of Grade 12 girls.

There are many different social groups within the school and if you are not friends with certain people then you are not involved with any of the school committees.
(Grade 12 girl, Nova Scotia)

For a school to have success in clubs it needs patriotism and school moral as a strong backbone of the school. The students would then enjoy coming to school and take pride in it, not show disrespect by littering or vandalizing. This moral could be generated maybe through closer association of the students making 'one big happy family', instead of niches of basketball players, volleyball players, and non athletic people such as drama, chess, or bowling groups.
(Grade 12 girl, New Brunswick)

As noted by different students, (see section on "student groups" in Chapter 5), such student groupings in the school may have an impact of the pattern and content of the joking relationships that develop among students.

School Size

An earlier analysis of students' views of schooling in Newfoundland and Labrador suggests that school spirit may be affected by the size of the school (Martin and Spain, 1986:20-44). The present study of students' observations of schooling in Atlantic Canada also indicate that this may be so. However, while is it generally reported that small schools tend to have a more positive school spirit, there are conflicting views on the advantage of small versus large school in this regard. To illustrate, a Grade 12 girl from Nova Scotia highlighted what she perceived to be a disadvantage of small schools:

> The school is small and gossip is spread very fast. I don't like that because if something happens in one class it carries over into the other classes. The teachers always talk it over and the students too, so it makes the act hard to live down.

A Grade 12 boy in New Brunswick was pleased with the friendliness of the teachers in his small school:

> I find that in small schools such as this the teachers are a lot more friendlier that in larger schools. They are more personal, and it really does make a difference to them whether you pass or not.

Similarly, a Grade 10 New Brunswick girl, after rating her school as "one of the best", reported that her school was "a small school and you get to know everyone". This line of thought is also seen in the comments of a Grade 11 girl who had moved from a small to a larger school in New Brunswick. After complaining that the "school spirit" at her present "school is DEAD", she wrote:

> I suppose I am being prejudiced, I am use to a small town school, but I it seems that the relationships between student and teacher at this school are somewhat distant. It is this way because of both student and teacher. Teachers have to let their hair down and become loose once in a while.

69

It should be noted that not all students believed that large schools are not conducive to the development of a school spirit. For example, one New Brunswick student, a Grade 11 girl, reported that "with 1500 students we have a great school spirit and most of the teachers are not just good teachers but nice people too".

Other observations relating to how school size may influence school spirit include:

I have attended different schools and I have found that the smaller the school is, the more personal it is and it provides a chance for better student-teacher relationships.
(Grade 11 girl, Nova Scotia)

The way in which our school is run is very good. The teachers are very friendly and are willing to help any one of the students. Since we are just a small school we have this one-to-one relationship with the teachers. I think it is very good to have a relationship like that.
(Grade 12 girl, New Brunswick)

I feel schools are too impersonal. They just seem to want you to pass and get on. You are not in close contact with your teachers, you don't know them or their lives. I feel these big schools cause you to lose contact with your teachers, which is very necessary to me.
(Grade 9 boy, Newfoundland and Labrador)

As far as teachers I think it's great to go to a small school because you get to know the teachers on a one-to-one basis and you get along better. I think it makes school more fun when you can joke around with your teachers without getting kicked out of class.
(Grade 12 boy, New Brunswick)

Clearly there is disagreement among students regarding the impact of school size on school spirit, perceived by many students as relevant joking relationship, but many are convinced that smaller schools are more likely than larger ones to display the type of school spirit that would support joking relationships.

CHAPTER 4

JOKING IN THE CLASSROOM

Based on the formal organization of the classroom, there are two general types of joking relationship: one between teacher and student and the other among students themselves. Focusing on joking in teacher-student interaction, students have highlighted the extent to which the humour is reciprocal. Also, they have observed that they use humour to break the monotony that sometimes characterizes teacher-student interaction. The negative consequences of teacher-initiated humour is also of major concern to some students, and the proliferation of boring jokes on the part of some teachers caught the attention of different students.

Reciprocity in Joking Relationships

There is a widely held view among high school students in each of the four Atlantic provinces that students should have more respect for their teachers than is often the case, and teachers should reciprocate with respect for their students. Earlier published comments on the helpful, co-operative and understanding nature of teacher-initiated relationships with their students in Newfoundland and Labrador schools illustrate the positive meanings which students give to such relationships (Martin, 1983). Similar observations were made by students in other Atlantic Canada schools. For example, one Grade 10 boy from New Brunswick wrote:

> I think that it is great for teachers and students to get along on
> and off duty. The teachers and principal here have a lot of
> respect for the students and vice-versa. It is good to love a
> teacher-student relationship. The school and students get

involved in a lot of activities and I think that is great
considering your grades are up. All in all I think this school is
the best.

Another student, a Grade 12 girl in the same New Brunswick school, complained:

Some teachers feel that since they are the teacher and we are the
students that they hold something over our heads and they can
criticize, insult and voice any opinion they have towards us, but
the system is not vice versa. Students have no rights in school.

Similarly, a Grade 11 girl in Newfoundland and Labrador opined that one of her teachers

"expects students to respect him when he gives no respect in return". A New Brunswick

student, a Grade 11 boy, advised teachers "to respect students a little more", and to

"understand" that students are still "growing... before they take action" against them. Other

students think that students themselves may be at fault in teachers lack of respect for their

charges. As put by a Grade 11 boy in Nova Scotia, "If you treat the teachers bad they will

reflect the same thing." The complexity of the nature of teacher-student relationships is

illustrated further by the Newfoundland Grade 10 boy who wrote:

Some teachers let the students off with too much fooling around.
The students carry the fooling around too far and the teacher
gets mad... The student blames the teacher. But it is not
teachers fault it is the students fault for carrying the fooling
around too far.

Focusing more specifically on student references to reciprocity in the joking

relationships in teacher-student interactions, a Grade 11 girl in Newfoundland and Labrador

wrote: "I appreciate it when teachers can joke with students and take a joke as well."

Similarly, a Grade 10 boy in another Newfoundland and Labrador school evaluated his

teachers as "all right" because "you can joke around with them".

The positive orientation which a Grade 10 boy in New Brunswick has toward one of his teacher who "can take a joke" is contrasted with his view of another of his teachers in his report:

> Most of the teachers I have can take a joke, my shop teachers
> and I get along real good, my carpenter teacher is like a friend
> to me, but my math teacher is another story.

A similar view was echoed by the Grade 9 Newfoundland boy who named one teacher who "don't mind a joke every now and then" while "all the other teachers would hang you" for attempting to joke with them.

Other students expressed their view that some teachers do not reciprocate student attempts to pursue humour related actions in student-teacher interactions:

> I feel the teachers are very good sometimes. Sometimes you
> can say something to be funny and get a laugh, the teachers take
> it seriously and you find yourself out in the hall.
> (Grade 9 boy, Newfoundland and Labrador)

> ... another thing about our school every time we tell the teacher
> a joke he will come down and beat our arms.
> (Grade 9 boy, Newfoundland and Labrador)

> We have a rule in this school about being friendly which says:
> Mingle with the other students; talk to them; smile at other
> people.... Often, when I smile at a teacher he doesn't smile
> back. I don't think this rule is fair because very often the
> teachers don't do their part.
> (Grade 10 girl, New Brunswick - translated from French)

Student perceived consequences of teachers not reciprocating their attempts to make humour a part of student-teacher interactions were noted by different students in the present research:

> I feel our school is an adequate institute for becoming educated.
> I feel all teachers do not like me because sometimes I make a

joke in the class to break the monotony although my marks are
in the eighties.
(Grade 11 boy, Nova Scotia)

Some of the teachers are too strict. Some never hardly smile
and if you just say something funny, they get mad.
(Grade 10 girl, Newfoundland and Labrador)

As noted by a Grade 11 girl in Newfoundland and Labrador, students should

keep their "side of the bargain" if they want to "laugh and have a good time" on occasion in

the school:

> The thing I like about this school is that if you are tired of
> working and you want to talk about other things for a while,
> most of the teachers will give you a break, we laugh and have a
> good time, but then you have to keep your side of the bargain
> and do your work & study. That's why I love school, because
> there are teachers, I can't say they are no good, because they
> help you allot even when you are down or upset they make sure
> you feel better.

Students' comments about the "boring jokes" which teachers bring to the

classroom suggest that students do not always respond to teacher initiated humour in a

manner that may be desired by the teacher (See section on "boring jokes" later in this

chapter).

Very likely there are a number of issues relating to the reciprocity in the

joking relationship among students themselves. One such issue is raised in the comments of

a Grade 11 New Brunswick girl, who draws attention to the unfairness that might arise when

students do not engage in reciprocity:

> Teachers should understand the student when they do something
> wrong. I put butter in someone's hair one and half months ago
> for her birthday and she went to the office. The Vice- Principle
> made her tell who did it and I got into 'shit' because I did that.
> About a week before someone got me for my birthday and she

74

got my pants, shirt, coat and hair and I didn't say a word to no
one.

Benefits of Classroom Humour

An earlier analysis of comments of high school students in Atlantic Canada

identified the monotony of teacher strategies to include "dullness", "passivity", "abundance

of teacher talk", "spoonfeeding" and requirements regarding memorization (Baksh and

Martin, 1986:117-123). As a response to this monotony, it is not uncommon to find students

suggesting the need for variety in teaching strategies which would include new and

challenging activities (Baksh and Martin, 1986:123-130). Among the teaching strategies

suggested by students is the need for teachers to inject humour into the teaching to break the

monotony of classroom life.

The injection of humour into classroom interaction is thought likely to produce

a variety of benefits. If teachers were "to get a little humour into the air", in the words of a

Grade 9 New Brunswick boy, it would enable them "to put themselves dow" to the students'

level, thus facilitating an improved relationship with their students. On the whole, a

teacher's inclination to introduce humour seems likely to generate a positive student attitude

toward him/her. A Grade 9 boy in Prince Edward Island, for example, claims to "like a

teacher who can have a good laugh once in a while with the class" and "does not always

stick to work all the time", while a Grade 9 boy from that province admits to liking teachers

who "joke around" a bit.

The use of humour by teachers is viewed as having other potential benefits. It

might help to stimulate or maintain student interest in the lesson:

Teachers should have better way of getting important things
across to the students and perhaps by using humor or other
techniques to get the class interested in what they are doing.
(Grade 11 boy, Newfoundland and Labrador)

Some of the teaching methods are not very effective in that the
teacher doesn't really get the student involved in the work. One
teacher in this school uses humor to get the student interested in
the subject, and most of the students are doing well in that
subject, while most other teachers just stand in front of the class
and 'teach'. They keep repeating information and writing notes
until the subject is driven into the students' brains. This causes
the subject to become boring and uninteresting to the student,....
(Grade 10 boy, Newfoundland and Labrador)

One thing that I feel has a great effect on a student is the
teachers attitude toward school. A student may want to learn
more easily if a teacher sometimes has a laugh with the class,
breaks from doing the same sort of thing day to day sometimes,
and has new things to do, that raise interest in the classroom.
(Grade 9 boy, Nova Scotia)

I feel that the majority of teachers are just teaching the class for
the sake of getting paid for it. However, some teachers do go
out of their way to make class more interesting. Jus by adding
a humorous remark in the middle of class can make a class
more interesting.
(Grade 10 girl, Nova Scotia)

The best teachers are able to communicate with a class and have
a sense of humor about what they do and teach. In that way,
they keep the classes attention and interest. If handled properly,
all students are capable of working hard and being obedient.
(Grade 12 boy, New Brunswick)

It might help make learning seem like fun:

Out teachers are easy going and give us the most important
notes. Their classroom behaviour is usually relaxed, sometimes
funny, and always fairly enjoyable. Some of our teachers mix
comedy in with their teaching routine, making for a relaxed
class, where you still learn but its not grind, grind, grind.

Others make sure they're work is completed and then maybe a
few laughs which I think is good.
(Grade 10 boy, Newfoundland and Labrador)

Teachers should have a good time during class. This makes it
fun for everybody even the teachers will be more relaxed and
feel better about his or her work.
(Grade 10 boy, Nova Scotia)

In the school the teachers should make the learning fun. Joke about some
things.
(Grade 10 girl, New Brunswick)

It might enhance student-teacher relationships:

I really do like all the teachers here and get along with most of
them well, there are a few exceptions such as not really
knowing them and not really trying to either. I feel this should
be the way between teachers and students so that you know if
they really are concerned about you, that you always have
somebody there to talk to, whether it be problems of some kind
or just to share a joke with and have a good laugh.
(Grade 12 boy, New Brunswick)

As for the environment around (this school) it is very good,
some teachers joke around and you feel like your at home, other
teachers aren't so liked.
(Grade 11 boy, New Brunswick)

Their are some teachers that I hate they don't give me a chance
to correct errors. They are always down your back, although
their is one teacher that I like. This is because he has nice long
talks with the class about problems that you will have to face in
life and he jokes around a bit....
(Grade 9 boy, Newfoundland and Labrador)

It might contribute to student enjoyment of what is being taught, perhaps even inducing a

liking for the subject:

I find some teachers are interesting and make you like what you
are learning. They do this by keeping you busy and by keeping
a good sense of humour most of the time.
(Grade 11 boy, Newfoundland and Labrador)

77

> I like math the most because I find that I understand all or most
> of the work we do. Another reason I like Math is because we
> have a teacher with a good sense of humour, which I think is a
> very important quality in teachers.
> (Grade 10 boy, New Brunswick)

It might also make learning an easier task:

> I think that most of the teachers in school are fairly likable but
> some are unbearable. It's as if they never seem to want to
> understand anything from your point of view. The periods are
> too long after 35 minutes you get so bored its hard to stay
> awake. I'm not saying that all classes are boring but sometimes
> they are. Usually they are quite amusing and it is easy to learn.
> If teachers knew how to reach us students, the work would be
> easier to learn.
> (Grade 10 boy, New Brunswick)

> I like the teachers who can take a joke and who'll let us have
> fun but still teach us a lot. I think we learn a lot better and a
> lot more.
> (Grade 9 girl, Prince Edward Island)

> Most of the teachers make learning a lot easier by relieving the
> tension in the classroom. They tell a joke or do something
> comical.
> (Grade 11 boy, Newfoundland and Labrador)

Negative Consequences of Humour

Students identified several negative consequences of different varieties of

classroom humour, including students' "joking around", teachers' "making fun of students",

students' "making fun of" each other, and teachers' "laughing at" students. The substantive

issues noted in students' comments are (1) the waste of time associated with joking around

and (2) student hesitancy to become more actively involved in classroom situations because

they fear being the butt of teacher and student jokes.

78

A Waste of Time

According to a relatively small number of students, what should be valuable teaching-learning time is sometimes wasted by teachers who are "always telling stories" and "jokes". A larger number of students claimed that teaching-learning time was lost because of student antics. While the students who initiated such behaviours may have thought it to be "funny", others had a different meaning for it. In addition to interfering with their own learning such behaviours are often seen to be disruptive to the overall teaching and learning processes in the school.

Waste of Time by Teachers

While the claim of one Grade 11 girl in Newfoundland and Labrador that teachers "often stray" from the subject "to talk about trivial things" reflects the views of many students in other provinces, only a few students specifically complained that teachers wasted time by telling jokes and pursuing other humour related actions. To quote two students representing an equal number of schools in Newfoundland and Labrador,

> This school has a couple of teachers which are slack and jokes
> around in the class too much and never gives you any notes,...
> (Grade 9 boy)

> Some teachers in this school are not very good. For example,
> some of my teachers carry on a lot they tell jokes,. ...
> (Grade 11 boy)

One Grade 9 boy in a third school in Newfoundland claimed that "there are some teachers who ... only come in class ... to have a laugh and to tell jokes". Another Grade 9 boy in this province linked excessive teacher humour with "slackness" and a wastage of class time; he described as "slack" a "couple of teachers" in his school "which jokes around in class too much and never gives you any notes". A third Grade 9 Newfoundland boy expressed his liking for "teachers who talk openly and joke now and then" and his distaste for "a teacher who tells jokes and makes fun all the time". In a similar vein, a girl, in the same grade and school, expressed the view that while some teachers "are always joking" other teachers "say there is a time for joking and a time for" being serious with students. A Grade 9 girl in another Newfoundland and Labrador school expressed the view that even though "school is a place where people come to learn", some students "just come for a joke", thereby wasting their time as well as that of others.

Comments from students in provinces other than Newfoundland and Labrador also suggest that time is sometimes wasted by teachers who tell stories and jokes:

> The teachers that we have all of us get along with them for helping us get a better education. Also some of the teachers here act real jerks. Their always laughing and telling sick jokes.
> (Grade 9 girl, New Brunswick)

> The teachers in this school are all nice, but sometimes they can be mean and most of the time they are all wasting time joking around with the students and teachers.
> (Grade 10 boy, New Brunswick)

> Sometimes they (teachers) just ramble on about things which don't even have anything to do with the subject being taught... They joke and laugh at the silliest things.
> (Grade 10 girl, Nova Scotia)

> As I see it the school is a sort of circus. When that bell rings people go wild in the halls. When we are in class the teachers are the clowns there to entertain us.
> (Grade 12 boy, Nova Scotia)

A Grade 10 Nova Scotia girl associates an excessive use of humour with immaturity and warns that "teachers should act mature and not joke around all the time".

Waste of Time by Students

A widespread complaint among high school students in each of the four Atlantic provinces is that there are students who disrupt the teaching-learning processes in the school. While some of their negatively oriented behaviours are not intended to be humorous, some of their actions are initiated in jest. After complaining that there is too much homework and not as many school buses as there "should be" and noting the need for more lockers in the school, a Grade 11 girl in Prince Edward Island wrote: "Another thing is when you are trying to do work in class and people are laughing at us."

It has been observed that some students "just come to school to have a good time" (Grade 9 girl, Newfoundland and Labrador), and consequently interfere with others who are more serious about getting an education. A Grade 12 girl in New Brunswick claimed that she failed Grade 9 because she "joked around and had a good time".
In addition to interfering with the academic efforts of others, students who are always trying to be funny sometimes "get others in trouble". As put by one Grade 9 boy in a Newfoundland and Labrador school,

> This school is pretty good but some of the students here are here
> for a laugh and they get others in trouble.

Other student complaints about their peers who became trouble makers with actions that involve one or another dimension of humour include the following:

> Being in the various classes throughout the school day, it gets
> pretty upsetting to see the people who think they are tough
> deliberately breaking the rules because they think they are cool
> and funny. Sometimes there are people who are hard to deal
> with when it comes to disciplining themselves. Suppose
> something important has to be done or someone is trying to talk
> (teacher) and all these people can do is be rude and talk as if

81

they were not even there letting the noise level gradually louder.
This really bugs me allot. If only we could show some of the
delinquents that grade 12 is where you start to become an adult
and it is no place for childish pranks, vandalism and other kinds
of foolishness.
(Grade 12 boy, New Brunswick)

In my class it is often quite hard to learn because there are some
students who think they have to make people laugh all the time.
(Grade 9 girl, New Brunswick)

The topic I would like to express is the behaviour of a
classroom. Most of the 'trouble makers' are the boys. They
come to class and do nothing but disturb the class when other
people are trying to learn. They come just to have a good time;
to carry on giggle and laugh; and because they are too young to
quit school. They should not be allowed to sauce back teachers
like they do and get away with it; that is what's wrong in our
school today. ... It's not that the books are too hard or the
teacher's are too strict, it's all student participation and the way
they act & treat the teachers.
(Grade 11 girl, Nova Scotia)

While blaming students for the disciplinary problems that were related to

actions with a humorous intent, a Grade 10 boy in New Brunswick reported that "some of

the teachers can't handle" the class she is in and "classroom is like a jungle" where

everyone is doing exactly what he/she wants to do. According to a number of students those

who disrupt the class, "thinking they are funny", should be kicked out the school:

I think school can be very enjoyable but it's the losers in the
school that wreck it. Always disrupting class, thinking they are
funny and that sort of thing. If we could get rid of them the
level of learning would go up considerably.
(Grade 11 boy, New Brunswick)

I feel the teachers in high school should only be here to teach
which is what they actually do. ... The teachers are here to
teach, the students to learn. When students begin to believe

82

school is a place to joke around then they should not remain
unless they have a seriousness towards receiving an education.
(Grade 12 boy, New Brunswick)

Our school wouldn't be that bad off if the teachers were more
strict. The students in our class act like idiots, laughing all the
time and the teacher only hollows at them instead of kicking
them out.
(Grade 11 girl, Nova Scotia)

One Grade 11 French student in New Brunswick suggested that all the time in

school should not be spent laughing:

School is a place where you study and where you learn to adapt
to society and to everyday life. School is not a place where you
spend all your time laughing. If you want to succeed in life,
you've got to make an effort.

The indications are that student gender may be a factor in situations where

students' attempts at humour result in disruptive behaviour. For example, girls from one or

more schools in each of the four provinces accused boys of creating discipline problems in

the school. Without reference to disciplinary problems as such, a Grade 9 girl in

Newfoundland and Labrador said that some of the boys "think they are real duds in school

but they are so stupid it's not even funny".

As seen from the student perspective, problems with student clowning are not

confined to the school environment. For example, after writing about the noise, the teasing,

the action of "clowns" on the school bus, a Grade 10 girl in Nova Scotia questioned why

other students should "suffer because of a bunch of clowns who can't behave properly."

Student Hesitancy

Although not a widespread feeling among the high school students participating

in the present research, comments were made to the effect that students have been hesitant in

83

taking a more active role in certain classroom situations because they were afraid that the teacher would "make fun of them". Students' concerns about teachers' actions which have been known to result in student embarrassment have been illustrated in an earlier book on Student Embarrassment which is based on the schooling experiences of students in Newfoundland and Labrador (Martin, 1985b). Focusing specifically on student hesitancy which is said to have been a result of teachers' laughing at them, it is may be noted that this cause and effect situation was not identified by any of the males in the present study. While by no means conclusive evidence of a gender difference in perception, it is interesting that all the observations regarding this particular effect of teachers' making fun of students come from female students. For example, a Grade 9 girl echoed the view of at least two other girls in her Grade in one Newfoundland school when she claimed: "Some teachers laugh at me if I try to express my feelings or try to prove a point." To further elaborate on this point of view, here are comments from Grade 12 girls in one Nova Scotia school:

> I feel that in order for a person to feel that he/she belongs or to have a fulfilling school life one must be encouraged to form and participate in other activities besides studying, etc. I feel that it is absolutely imperative that teachers encourage students for if they do not and in this there is one particular teacher who even goes so far as to discourage students from partaking in extra curricular events and organizations, the students will lose all interest. I feel that students should be able to express individuality in and out of the classroom and not to be mocked for expressing their individuality.

> I think that teachers should care more about the individual who needs help. Most of the study time in class is spent swapping ideas with the classroom 'brain' and the student who does not understand something has to fend for himself. I realize that these students could ask the teacher to help, but are afraid that the teacher or other students will make fun of them. This happens a lot and a student ends up failing a course.

A Grade 12 Nova Scotia girl expressed her view on the consequences of having teachers who "laugh at" students when she wrote:

> Some teachers seem to actually enjoy humiliating a student in front of other students which can have a terrible effect on younger students. This makes them lose their self-confidence in school and other areas. From my experience with teachers that laugh at you and try to embarrass or humiliate you, I hardly ever ask a question in class or even try and get to know most teachers.

The opinion of one Grade 10 girl in Newfoundland was that such teacher initiated humour revolved around academic performance:

> One thing which really gets to me is the way the students relate to other students. When a person does well in a text he/she gets laughed at by the rest. Their are many students in this school who could do really well only they are afraid to because they will be laughed at by their friends.

Stupid Jokes

Students from a number of schools observed that teachers are not always successful in their "telling jokes" with the intention of adding humour to the classroom. On the contrary, their jokes are often perceived by the students to be "stupid" and tend not to get the teachers' desired effect. For example, a Grade 9 boy in one Newfoundland school wrote: "Some teachers tell the driest and the more boring jokes, so many times it makes you sick," while a Grade 11 girl in another Newfoundland and Labrador school complained that her "teachers tell boring jokes" which are "dry and uninteresting". A New Brunswick boy in Grade 10 blamed his teachers, who allegedly "act as if they are dried up" with their "teaching and jokes" for school, for being "boring sometimes". Here are the comments of three students from one Newfoundland and Labrador school:

85

> ... teaches us History and makes it very boring. He also tells
> the horrible dry jokes. (Grade 9 boy)

> The History teacher is dumb. He gets in front of the class
> telling dry jokes and insulting students. (Grade 9 boy)

> Most teachers are boring, they tell dry jokes and you can't
> understand the teacher at all. (Grade 10 girl)

A Grade 10 boy in New Brunswick argued that a teacher cannot make class

"interesting" with "boring jokes". A Grade 10 girl in Nova Scotia wrote:

> Most teachers make their classes interesting and their classes are
> the classes that I like to go to. But some of my teachers make
> their classes boring with jokes and by the end of the class, I am
> ready to go to sleep.

The subject of the stupid jokes of one of his teachers was identified by one

Newfoundland boy in Grade 9 as "religion". The student wrote that his teacher "is ignorant"

and "tells religious jokes". A Grade 10 girl in New Brunswick was upset because "there are

also teachers in" her "school who talk and joke more about what they did the night before

than they do about the subject." Another Grade 10 girl in a second New Brunswick school

noted that her "teachers are mostly boring because" she "cannot understand their stupid

jokes". In the view of one Grade 10 boy in New Brunswick, one of his male teachers tells

"dirty boring jokes" which are not appreciated by his classes.

The suggestion was made by one Prince Edward Island student that teachers

who "try to be funny" by telling jokes are not usually successful in getting "laughs from

many students". In contrast to this view, a Grade 9 girl in New Brunswick observed that all

teachers do have, and need to have, a sense of humour. But, what really bothers her is

having "teachers with no sense of humour... who think they're funny when really they are

86

pathetic". Similarly, the pitfalls in teacher exploitation of humour as a classroom technique were suggested by a Grade 9 boy from New Brunswick who pointed to the futility of teachers' trying "to be funny" when they are unable to be truly amusing, a situation that usually results in their making "stupid jokes" and thus earning their students' contempt.

CHAPTER 5

INDIVIDUAL CHARACTERISTICS AND
GROUP PROCESSES

Students in each of the four Atlantic provinces observed that humour can be an important element in what constitutes an "a good teacher". Also, a significant number of student comments relating to school humour identify teacher age and student maturity as having an effect on the extent and nature of humour in the classroom. Another, and interrelated, category of student comments refers to the presence of groups among teachers and within the student body which also seem to be important in the development of humour in teacher-student interactions.

Humorous versus Serious Teachers

It is obvious that many students would argue that teachers who employ humour in their teaching are often serious about the teaching-learning endeavour in the classroom. In fact, they are sometimes perceived to be more serious and concerned about student welfare and learning than teachers who are "serious" in the sense of being authoritarian and stern. By way of presenting student comments which address the issues of humorous versus serious teachers, serious in the sense of appearing stern and "grum", it is convenient to divide them into four sets: one set identifies humour as an important characteristic in good teaching, a second contains complaints about teachers who are always serious, a third are students' comparisons of humorous and serious teachers, and a fourth are observations that some teachers combine humour with sternness in their teaching.

A Characteristic of Good Teachers

Students in the present study identified a number of characteristics of a good teacher. For example, a Grade 11 boy in Newfoundland and Labrador wrote:

I feel that teachers give too much freedom to the students. I believe a good teacher is someone who is strict, assigns homework, makes little jokes in class, is well dressed, has a good attitude towards the students. I also believe that if a student wants to work ahead the teacher should offer some assistance to the individual if they need it. I also believe that teachers should get papers or assignments corrected as fast as possible.

Focusing on the topic at hand, a diverse sample of students indicated that one of the major characteristics of most good teachers is that they have "a sense of humour" and "crack a joke".

.... In order to be a good teacher, I think that they should have a good sense of humor. A few laughs now and then seems to make people feel much more comfortable and able to speak up.
(Grade 11 girl, Newfoundland and Labrador)

If a teacher really wants to his students to enjoy his classes and be interested in them, he has to relax a little and maybe crack a joke or something.
(Grade 11 girl, Newfoundland and Labrador)

The thing I expect from a teacher is that it is someone who gets along with kids, has patience, lets the student carry a joke as long as it is not carried too far....
(Grade 9 boy, Newfoundland and Labrador)

For teachers - they should like kids, know how to handle them and most of all have a 'good' sense of humor.
(Grade 9 girl, New Brunswick)

The influence of teachers' joking relationship with students on students' attitudes toward their teachers was alluded to by different students. Students tend to like a

89

teacher who is seen as one who "jokes around", especially when other characteristics, such

as teachers treating their "students like adults", are found in teacher-student relationships:

> Many of the teachers are well liked because they most students
> like adults. Some teachers are also known to joke around and
> some tell a few jokes. This adds to the excitement of the class.
> Also it keeps the attention of the students.
> (Grade 12 boy, New Brunswick)

> I feel the only way a student will like a teacher is that the
> teacher would joke around a little and not take the serious role
> of an old miser.
> (Grade 10 boy, New Brunswick)

> I like all the teachers that I have because they are always there
> to help me when I have a problem, and they are not boring we
> have a laugh in class.
> (Grade 9 girl, Newfoundland and Labrador)

> Some teacher don't behave badly. They make students laugh
> when they are funny in some ways such as telling jokes, riddles
> and stories....
> (Grade 9 girl, Newfoundland and Labrador)

> Well, I can usually tell if he/she is a good teacher. If he/she is
> terribly teacher then I get bored. And I like teachers who joke
> around a bit when they come in through the door. I seem to
> come alive and recover from the class.
> (Grade 10 boy, Newfoundland and Labrador)

Teachers who joke with their students create positive attitudes towards

themselves but, it has been suggested, this strategy gives students a greater desire to be in

the classroom and an incentive to stay in school. It has also been claimed that students

would even "learn more quickly and remember it longer" if humour was employed in the

teaching process:

> I have my favourite teachers and classes because of the
> atmosphere. It's fun to laugh while learning because it makes a

90

student (well it does me anyway) want to be in the class with
the teacher and learn more.
(Grade 11 girl, New Brunswick)

.... Teachers wonder why we don't like school. We would if
they might at least laugh once or twice a week.
(Grade 11 girl, New Brunswick)

If the teachers made classes fun then I think a lot less people
would skip and more would enjoy classes. Also, if classes were
fun, the students would learn more quickly and remember it
longer.
(Grade 11 girl, Prince Edward Island)

Some students were of the opinion that while a sense of humour is an

important dimension of most situations, the teaching and learning of some subjects does not

require such a teaching strategy:

A little humour helps in some classes whereas others such as
math I find a straight forward and confident teacher helps. The
confidence a teacher has lets a student have the respect that is
needed in a High School, where it seems the teachers are almost
as young as the students.
(Grade 11 girl, New Brunswick)

However, other students suggested that humour is subject bound in that it can be successfully

employed while teaching a broad range of subjects. For example, a Grade 10 girl in

Newfoundland and Labrador implied that her "geometry teacher is a good teacher" because

"he has a sense of humor, and helps you when you need it". After claiming that "all" her

"teachers are very good", a Grade 12 girl in Nova Scotia reports "they make their classes

interesting and funny, especially English and Physics".

A Less Desirable Teacher Characteristic

Changing the focus from students' comments which highlight the belief that a

sense of humour is an important teacher characteristic to students' comments which address

91

the stern and serious nature of teachers, one finds a different tone of expression. Observations on the seriousness of teachers, serious meaning not humorous, are more often than not offered in a complaining voice:

> This school is pretty good but some of the teachers don't have a
> sense of humor they are always so serious.
> Grade 9 boy, Newfoundland and Labrador)

Just as students tend to like teachers with a sense of humour, they tend to dislike those whom they perceive to be too serious. Those teachers are often thought boring. As put by a Grade 11 New Brunswick boy, "some of my teachers I do dislike... ones who bore you with endless facts and no fun." A Grade 10 girl in Nova Scotia complained that her teachers are "so boring" and "always serious" that they "would crack in half if they ever smiled". Similarly, after reporting that her "algebra class is very boring" and the "teacher never cracks a smile", a Grade 9 Newfoundland girl wrote: "If I ever see him smile in class I might faint."

On occasion, students have equated "serious" teachers and those who are "mad all the time". In the words of one Grade 11 girl in Newfoundland and Labrador, "...the teachers are too serious and mad at their class all the time." A Grade 10 boy in New Brunswick observed that "some" teachers "are always down your back, they never smile". When a teacher or a principal is perceived to be too serious, he/she is often seen to be "too strict":

> Principal - wants to run a military school. Gets alot of good
> things for us but has no sense of humour. He is too strict.
> (Grade 11 girl, Newfoundland and Labrador)

92

In my opinion school is alright but the teachers are too strict.
The principal is not good enough to us. He never talks to us,
he never smiles.
(Grade 9 girl, New Brunswick - translated from French)

Comparing Teachers

It is not surprising that the process of comparing one teacher to another is
widespread among high school students in Atlantic Canada. One of the many things which
they use to make much comparisons is the teacher's location on a continuum that ranges
from the presence of a good sense of humour all the time to the complete absence of any
sense of humour. In the later case, teachers are perceived to be "always serious", stern and
authoritarian. To illustrate, here are some of the students' comments in comparing teachers
on this aspect of teacher-student relationships:

The teachers should try and make a class fun, some teachers do
but some would make you fall asleep.
(Grade 12 girl, Prince Edward Island)

You have your real good teachers who you really respect, you
have some really funny teachers which are good and also
relaxing, but you have those that are bossy,... always serious..
and a real pain.
(Grade 12 girl, Prince Edward Island)

The only thing I don't really like in our school is that some of
the teachers just get up there and talk or write on the board. If
you want to get things through to a student you should be
interesting and some teachers are. Some of them get up there
and talk about there subjects and make jokes or do something to
keep the students interested.
(Grade 11 boy, New Brunswick)

I like school and some of the teachers. The ones I like are jolly
and act a fool but get their job done.
(Grade 11 girl, New Brunswick)

93

The teachers are, for the most part interesting, although some
can be boring enough to put you to sleep because they look so
serious all the time....
(Grade 10 girl, New Brunswick)

Because myself and my friends like to have fun, some of my
teachers punish us but they call us immature, and attention
getters. This really isn't fair because we aren't doing any harm.
Sure we may be disruptive at times, but teachers should expect
they will never have a perfect class. Then again there are some
of my teachers who have a really good sense of humour, they
joke around with us, and we find that we get better marks and
get along with that teacher a lot better.
(Grade 12 girl, New Brunswick)

Most of the teachers are reasonable, willing to listen to our
views, but they seldom take our suggestions seriously. Some
teachers are not as good as others because they are not as open-
minded, they run their classroom almost like a dictatorship.
This makes for boring and unamusing classes. I find that the
teachers who will discuss things gain 'respect' not just 'fear'
from their students.
(Grade 10 boy, New Brunswick)

...it would be nice if you could walk into a classroom and see a
nice big smile on a teacher's face, some here are like that but
others aren't....
(Grade 10 girl, Newfoundland and Labrador)

Some teachers are all right and are funny and have a few
laughs, but others are boring and strict.
(Grade 9 girl, Newfoundland and Labrador)

I think that some of the teachers in the school are too bossy.
Some of them think they have full control of everything. ....
On the other hand, some teachers are good and act like a person
should. Some joke and smile while others are too grumpy to
have anything to do with.
(Grade 11 boy, Newfoundland and Labrador)

Some teachers are that boring that you get not to like the subject
very much and because you don't like the subject you might not

get very high marks. But there are some teachers that you can
joke around with and they won't get mad.
(Grade 9 girl, Newfoundland and Labrador)

Some teachers that have taught me good and I learned alot. One
was serious in class and did not let us joke around all the time.
But other teachers would come in, let us say for religion, and
we would end up talking about fish, the teacher's life and telling
jokes.
(Grade 10 girl, Newfoundland and Labrador)

Some teachers will punish you for dropping your pencil and
other teachers will joke about it.
(Grade 9 girl, Nova Scotia)

Combining Humour and Seriousness

While some high school students often give the impression that they want

teachers to be joking all the time and other students complain about their teachers' lack of a

sense of humour, most students apparently want to see teachers use a combination of humour

and more solemn strategies in their teaching. Without referring to humour, as such, a Nova

Scotia girl in Grade 12 may have been thinking of humour as a human and social aspect of

teaching when she wrote:

Teachers who combine human and social aspects of life with
their subjects seem to captivate and hold the students interest
more than the teacher who teaches the mechanics of the subject,
not livening it up.

Students' satisfaction with the combination of "humour" and seriousness is

evidenced in the following sample of their comments:

The teachers of this school are the best. They are good sports
which helps the students, they joke at times and are serious at
other times. We couldn't ask for a better staff.
(Grade 11 girl, Newfoundland and Labrador)

95

(Teachers) classroom behavior is usually relaxed, sometimes
funny, and always enjoyable. .... Some of our teachers mix
comedy in with their teaching routine, making for a relaxed
class, where you still learn but its not grind, grind, grind.
Others make sure their work is completed and then maybe a few
laughs which I think is good
Grade 10 boy, Newfoundland and Labrador)

There's good student-teacher relationship in and out of classes,
not serious all the time.
(Grade 12 girl, Prince Edward Island)

I have almost no complaints about our school. The teachers are
not strict, they joke in class but have a serious side too. I
say we are pretty well off and couldn't get much better.
(Grade 11 boy New Brunswick)

Most of the teachers here are decent. They are a few who I've
really enjoyed. These teachers are funny and they enjoy having
a laugh. They aren't so serious all the time.
(Grade 11 girl, Nova Scotia)

In addition to references to the need for balance between humour and other

strategies in teacher-student relationships, different students suggested that when students "act

like responsible people" they are not "carrying on" or "fooling around... all the time".

There is room for "fun and games", but in order for students to make anything of

themselves, they "must be serious" in their school work.

Age in the Classroom

There are two dimensions of age in the classroom which seem to be associated

with students' perceptions of the extent of humour in this setting. One dimension is whether

the teachers are seen to be "young" or "old" and the other is the student definition of their

level of students' maturity.

Young versus Old Teachers

The age of their teachers as well as the student perceived length of time they are teaching tend to be a major concern of students in each of the four Atlantic provinces. A small number of students complained that their new teachers did not have the sense of humour of the older. To quote from one Grade 10 boy in Newfoundland,

> In this school there are too many new teachers coming in every year, and most of them do not know how to teach. Our old ones were good teachers and had a sense of humour. These new ones obey all rules and don't know how to teach worth crap.

A more common complaint among high school students in Atlantic Canada is that their teachers are "too old" and have been teaching so long that they have lost whatever sense of humour they might have had earlier in their careers:

> We have a math teacher that looks like a teacher from 'the little red school house days', always strict and a serious look all the time.
> (Grade 10 boy, New Brunswick)

> This school is not all that bad, however as with everything there is room for improvement. For one thing I don't think that some of the teachers here should be teaching. A few of them are growing older, and it becomes very difficult to deal with their bad moods, no jokes and constant discouragement.
> (Grade 12 girl, New Brunswick)

After complaining about teachers who they think are too old to teach or to introduce humour into the classroom, some students suggested that those teachers should try to act younger and thereby relate better to the students:

> I personally feel that any school could help their students feel more at ease with the teacher. I have only one teacher like that and that's my band teacher. He acts and talks like sixteen year

97

old teenager than a man whose married and has 2 kids that are
both around seven years old.
(Grade 10 girl, Prince Edward Island)

Yet, in attempting to act younger than they are, teachers are sometimes

perceived to be "childish". It has also been observed that teachers are sometimes laughed at

when they act as if they are much younger than their years:

Some of the teachers are very childish. It is easy to see that
they need a class to dominate, it gives them a feeling of
superiority. This doesn't get a teacher anywhere, they're just
laughed at.
(Grade 12 girl, Prince Edward Island)

A Grade 11 New Brunswick boy observed that younger teachers tend to let

students control each other more so than do older ones:

I also think some of the older teachers rule with an iron hand.
They send you to the office every time you do something, ...
they don't understand that students will do the same thing over
and over again just to annoy them, just for the fun of doing it.
If a student is disrupting the teacher, Mr. ... who is younger
lets the other students handle it and usually the clown will calm
down.

One of the main reasons for the students' argument that many of the older

teachers in Atlantic Canada should be replaced with younger ones is the view that, compared

with their older counterparts, "younger teachers are easier to get along with" and they tend

to employ humour more often in their relationships with students. Here are some of the

comments students made expressing their preferences for younger teachers while claiming

that school is more fun and that one can joke with such teachers:

My teachers should be younger.... Young teachers are fun.
They are not warped like the old ones.
(Grade 11 girl, Nova Scotia)

I find the teachers we have are excellent. They are young and
eager and fun to go through school with.
(Grade 9 girls, Nova Scotia)

I think some of the older teachers should retire and let younger
more qualified teachers take their place. You can joke with
them.
(Grade 10 girl, Newfoundland)

I find that teachers should be up to date with the kids. The
older teachers shouldn't be around because they think in the
ways of being strict. The teachers should be just out of
university so they will be in the same time slot as kids and we
can understand their jokes.
(Grade 11 boy, Prince Edward Island)

I think that they should replace the old teachers and make room
for more young and excited ones.
(Grade 9 girl, Nova Scotia)

Student Maturity

A review of student observations on classroom humour and student maturity

suggests that there are at least three distinct views among high school students concerning

their level of maturity and teachers' actions toward them. An occasional student observed,

first, that the some of the students in their respective schools are "immature". Their

immaturity is evidenced by their "clowning" around and creating a disturbance with their

laughter.

Other students reported, secondly, that their teachers treat them like adults in

that they joke and laugh with them. For instance, one Grade 12 Prince Edward Island girl,

who claimed that the teachers in her school high expectations for the students, added that

"maybe that's why we have such a good school", one in which teachers "try to make"

students "reasonable and more adult like" as they talk and joke with their students. In contrast to the view that high school students are not treated as adults, which they perceive themselves to be, some high school students compared the treatment they received in high school with that they had experienced in junior school. For example, a Grade 10 girl in a Nova Scotia high school wrote:

> I think that the amount of freedom that is given to us is good because it encourages more students, who didn't have the chance before, to gain responsibilities. The junior high schools treat students more like children than young adults but this school makes you comfortable and more like adults. I think it makes the students feel better when they are treated like adults because it sure makes me happy,

A Grade 11 New Brunswick girl observed:

> Our teachers are alright people; most of them treat us like young adults rather than young people. Most of them have some kind of sense of humour and are o.k. outside of school.

Thirdly, there is a widespread view among high school students in Atlantic Canada that many of their teachers think of them as being less mature than they believe themselves to be. Consequently, students claim that their teachers do not joke or laugh with them. To illustrate, here are comments of a sample of students in the present research:

> The teacher in our school are alright when it comes to being qualified but one of the main problems I find is not being treated as an equal. Granted we may not be as accomplished as they are in some areas but I'm speaking about equality as a person. The way they talk to us they never crack a smile. No one appreciates being treated like a two year old in a teenagers body. I swear they keep us in such iron control because they are afraid if they don't any second we'll wet our pants and they will have to change our pampers.
> (Grade 10 girl, Nova Scotia)

> Another thing is the attitude of a few teachers toward their students. They treat us like kids, yet expect us to act like adults.

> By grade 11 and 12 if they still do that then they should be
> teaching elementary school where they never have a laugh.
> (Grade 11 boy, Nova Scotia)

> I find that the teachers here say that you should be reasonable,
> and sometimes they treat us like babies. Before I came to this
> school, I never had any problem with any of the teachers or
> with my grades. This year I get the feeling they're on my case.
> They think that just because I laugh in class from time to time
> that I'm a bad student. The teachers (some of them) are not fair
> toward the students.
> (Grade 10 girl, New Brunswick - translated from French))

> Teachers should realize people who are growing and maturing
> are passing through a very traumatic time and by playing an
> authoritarian role they are not helping the student.
> (Grade 12 girl, New Brunswick)

In contrast to the idea that when teachers treat students like adults there would be more humour in student-teacher relationships than would be the case if they did not, a Grade 11 boy in New Brunswick complained that his teachers "think that we as students should be like grown ups and never have any fun". Similarly, a Grade 10 boy in Nova Scotia wrote:

> The reason I like school is because when I leave I will be an
> adult and who wants to be that. I want to be a kid still living it
> up in school. Boy is it fun.

Maybe the Nova Scotia Grade 11 girl identified the problem faced by many teachers as they decide whether to treat their students as adults or children when she observed:

> Teachers are too different. One treats you like babies, the other
> like full grown adults, and really you are neither of these.

101

On occasion, students complain that some of their peer group act immaturely and as a result affect the student-student relationships in the school. To quote a Grade 11 girl in Newfoundland and Labrador,

> I sometimes wonder about the school system. Often I get very angry with other students (I try not to show it). They seem so immature all the time. They make fun and laugh at you. I often wish there was a class we could attend, if we thought it was necessary that help us to get along with others socially. Some of my fellow students act terribly selfish alot of the time (I realize that I seem that way to people sometimes too).

Teacher Gender

With reference to classroom humour, the issue of the gender of the teacher was raised by only a small number of students. One Grade 10 girl in New Brunswick complained that one of her male teachers "is really perverted" and "says gross things to the girls ... dirty jokes". A Grade 9 girl in Prince Edward Island expressed the view that "male teachers are more open" in school than female teachers are. She added that the male teachers "try to be funny and make the class worth learning". Male teachers have also been accused of showing favouritism in that they joke more with the girls than with the boys. To quote from the comments of one Grade 10 boy in New Brunswick,

> Teachers such as males, only certain ones, use favoritism, such as a male teacher favours girls and when they ask a question to a teacher he gives them all the help, but when you ask a question he will tell you to figure it out. Besides, he is always talking and laughing with the girls.

A Nova Scotia Grade 12 girl claimed that she was laughed at by a female teacher when she reported a problem to her. This student did not appreciate the lighthearted manner in which a female teacher responded to her problem:

A teacher, who is head of student police, screams and pushes the kids to their home rooms and will not allow us to get our books and therefore I am always late for my first class. A number of students, including myself, asked a teacher (woman) what we should do because he is very big and scares people with his screaming -- he's not the most pleasant person in the world to be greeted by at 8:51 each morning -- and she laughed. After she told us if we wanted any change made in the school to consult her -- and she laughed! Since then, I will never tell another teacher any problem that I might experience because I don't feel I could hold their trust.

Groups

As suggested by high school students' reports of their schooling experiences in Atlantic Canada, there are two dimensions of groups in the school which seem to be an influence on the extent and nature of school and classroom humour. One is the fact that students form groups among themselves and the other is the student view that a camaraderie sometimes develops within groups of teachers as they "make fun of" and "laugh at" particular aspects of students' identities.

Student Groups

Students from different schools in each of the four Atlantic provinces made reference to the presence of student groupings which have consequences for overall relationships within the school. Here is how one Grade 12 boy in New Brunswick put it:

School is broken up into cliques. If you don't belong to a group of people or having only friends, your school life can be very boring and lonesome. Having good friends is what helps to make school more enjoyable.

At the outset it should be realized that there are diverse opinions on the consequences of such groupings. For example, while one Grade 12 girl in Nova Scotia observed that even though "there are cliques in" her school, "mostly everyone gets along" because of a sense of "unity" the school, another Nova Scotia girl (Grade 10) in a different school, wrote: "There is also a big conflict between the 'jocks' and the 'band students' and I, being stuck in the middle, wish something could be done to change this."

As suggested by students' comments, there are joking relationships which are pursued in jest within a student group as well as more hostile jokes between one group and another. Obviously, there are many reasons why students form groupings among themselves within the school, and those reasons are interrelated with the joking relationships that develop within and among student groups. One factor that leads to the development of student groups is clothing:

> I feel that in my school, in particular, there is a certain group of people who treats others like dirt and I really hate the attitude that they take toward other people. If you do not wear the right kind of shoes, you get funny looks and so on. I am in this particular high school to learn and do well, I'm not here just because I want to belong to this certain group. What really makes me mad is when a person not so rich, walks by and he's wearing respectable clothes and this 'group' starts making wise cracks about what he's wearing. This is the most noticeable characteristic of this school and mostly the reason why our high school is often called the 'Snob school'.
> (Grade 11 girl, New Brunswick)

> Here I have noticed that peer pressure is very strong. It rules the way you dress, eat, talk, your general school life. If you don't wear the 'in' clothes, you become literally a social outcast.
> (Grade 9 girl, Prince Edward Island)

Student thoughts about themselves and as well as the way they behave have also been noted as important elements in the development of student groups:

> Our school has two sets of students and they don't mix. The ones who think their perfect and the ones who know their not.

104

...they laugh at each other.
(Grade 12 girl, Nova Scotia)

I feel that some teachers get along too good with students in the
way that students might play up to the teachers just to get better
marks which most of the time happens, while others on the
medium side of the teachers suffer because of this.
(Grade 9 boy, Newfoundland and Labrador)

I like coming to school and I also enjoy having lots of friends,
which I don't. I feel that most of the students in this school
think their better than I am. This makes me very upset. Hardly
anybody talks to me or hangs around with me. I do my best to
get them to like me but it just don't work.
(Grade 11 girl, New Brunswick)

Student age and size have also been identified as a variable in the development
of in-groups among students and the resultant joking relationships among them. For example,
a Grade 9 girl in Nova Scotia reported that she knew "of some girls who threaten younger,
smaller girls in" her school. She added that "bigger girls make fun of smaller ones" and
"are hurting younger ones and I don't think that is fair".

Other reasons for the development of groups among the students are seen in
the comment of this Grade 11 New Brunswick girl:

And over all I like this school except of course for the fact we
all seem to be put into groups, farmers, jocks band students and
then your group of none of the above. I wish our school would
respect the students for who they are, not by where they live
and what they like to do.

It has been noted that students in one group often make fun of those in
another. For example, a Grade 10 Newfoundland boy complained that "some students make
fun of other students and this causing them to loose interest in school." After reporting that
she likes her school, a Grade 10 girl in Nova Scotia added that she finds "it hard to get

105

involved in activities". She went on to write: "People in this school make fun of you if you try sports and are not good."

Teacher Groups

It is understandable, since it is a generally accepted dimension of school culture, for students think of themselves and their teachers in terms of "we" and "they". However, students become annoyed when they think that their teachers are gossiping and "laughing" at them "behind" their backs. While not a widespread phenomenon, a small number of students in a few schools scattered across the provinces expressed displeasure with this type of action. To elaborate, a Grade 9 girl in Nova Scotia wrote:

> ... another thing is that the teachers gossip in the staff room about their students, especially if they have done something wrong! It's a laugh for them.

After expressing her displeasure that "gossip is spread very fast"in her school, a Grade 12 girl from Nova Scotia observed:

> Also, teachers talk about our behavior, things will be slack for a while then all teachers will clamp right down. One knows they have gotten together and decided as a group what to do. I dislike that aspect of the school.

A Grade 10 girl in New Brunswick observed:

> I also find the teachers in this school are too noisy. All they do is talk or gossip about the students.

Another New Brunswick student wrote:

> This isn't a school but a prison, or a nursery school, and the teachers area real bunch of gossips. They tell what everyone is doing and then they laugh about the students because of the way they're dressed. (Translated from French).

Along similar lines of thought, a Prince Edward Island Grade 9 girl wrote:

> Most of the teachers... expect everyone in this school to be
> excellent students, but they're not. They all love to gossip and
> joke about the students in the staff room after school which I
> don't think they should.

Such remarks convey clearly students's displeasure at being the subjects of gossip among

their teachers.

CHAPTER 6

SOCIAL-EMOTIONAL DIMENSIONS
OF CLASSROOM HUMOUR

As evidenced by observations of a substantial number of students, representing a range of schools in each of the four Atlantic provinces, classroom humour is an important ingredient in the social-emotional well being of student life in this setting. The positive impact of different aspects of humour on teacher-student relationships and, consequently, on self and learning processes in the classroom, has been referred to in each of the preceding chapters. The present task is to review students' observations that suggest an association between classroom humour and such facets of classroom life as teachers' differential treatment of students, teachers' sarcasm and insult in dealing with students, making fun of students "in front of the class", and moods in the classroom.

Differential Treatment

A review of students' observations on schooling in Newfoundland and Labrador illustrated their view that many teachers often do not treat all students equally (Martin, 1982:6-17). They frequently referred to the contrasting phenomena of teachers' favouring particular students while mistreating or ignoring others. An analysis of comments from students in other Atlantic provinces suggest that, from their perspectives, the processes associated with teachers' pets and class victims are common to most high school classrooms in this part of the country. The consequences of this phenomena have been shown to include: students' feeling of being left out of much of the everyday teacher-student interactions; their perceptions that marks and the disciplinary process are influenced by

108

teachers' favouring-mistreating attitudes and actions; students' attitudes toward teachers; and

the development of antipathy and empathy among students (Martin, 1982:49-64; 1984). In

addition to these consequences, the present study highlights the influence of pets-victims

phenomena on classroom humour.

Pets

Similar to the findings in Newfoundland and Labrador (Martin, 1982;

1985c:32-43), students in each of the other three Atlantic provinces often reported the

presence of teachers' pets and the accompanying favouritism associated with this

phenomenon (which may be its identifying characteristics to begin with). Here is a sample

of their comments:

> I like most of my teachers, but there is some teachers who have
> their favorite students, and let them get away with anything and
> that makes me sick.
> (Grade 10 girl, Prince Edward Island)

> What makes me mad is that all teachers have pets. This isn't
> fair because it usually discourages other students.
> (Grade 10 girl, New Brunswick)

> The teachers always seem to have one favorite student and that
> bugs me. I feel it is unfair. In my class this year a couple of
> my teachers have pets who are either smart or snobby and I hate
> that.
> (Grade 10 girl, Nova Scotia)

> Some teachers favour other students in the classroom. I know
> other people have recognized this because I have talked to them
> about it. If a teacher does not favour anyone and treats the
> students the same, teacher and student relationships would be
> better.
> (Grade 12 girl, Nova Scotia)

In contrast to the number of students who reported that teachers favoured certain students, only a few students specifically noted that teachers "joke with" those students more than they do with others. One of those was a Grade 11 Nova Scotia girl, who, after reporting that she did not like the way "some teachers pick favourites" in the classroom, remarked that a teacher's tone of voice sometimes suggests that those who are not among the favourites "are made fun of" in their very presence. She scornfully expressed her dislike for this type of "joke", complaining that it was not "funny". The following observations illustrate the suggestion that teachers joke with their pets more often than with other students:

> I don't like it when teachers favour certain students and if they don't like you they show it, e.g., sometimes in marks or just by the way they treat you. They talk and joke with you.
> (Grade 10 girl, Prince Edward Island)

> I think all teachers have a pet or favourite person in every class. That person is in on the fun and jokes. I think that it's not fair because when one person does anything wrong they get in trouble. But if the pets do something wrong they don't get in trouble.
> (Grade 11 girl, Nova Scotia)

> I think teachers should have better relationships with their students. Not so impersonal. A laugh is good for you. Teachers should not have favorites or people they do not like.
> (Grade 11 girl, Nova Scotia)

> One thing I dislike are those teachers that pick 'pets' to talk to and smile at and don't really bother with their other students as much.
> (Grade 10 girl, New Brunswick)

But, given the nature of the interactions between teachers and their pets, as perceived by students, the suggestion here is that forms of humour other than "joking" could

110

be found more often in teacher-pet interactions than in teacher-victim interactions. However, as illustrated below interactions between teachers and victims may sometimes be characterized by sarcasm.

Victims

Just like some high school students in Newfoundland and Labrador (Martin, 1982:18-35; 1984; 1985c:32-43), a significant number of those participating in the present study in the rest of Atlantic Canada also reported that students are sometimes victimized because of their "intelligence", school/classroom behaviour, gender, place of residence, and family background. Focusing on classroom humour, it is noted that, compared to the relatively few student observations that teachers joke with their pets more often than they do with others in the classroom, there seems to be a widespread discontent with the way teachers "mistreat" and "neglect" certain students, thereby taking "the fun out of school". Students' comments in this regard include:

> Teachers pick on a student because they did not understand a question the first time, but the second time they did. There is no joy when the teacher carries this on for weeks afterward.
> (Grade 10 boy, New Brunswick)

> The teachers pick on the boys. In gym class the guys laugh at something and the teacher gives us a dirty look, but when the girls laugh or say something he laughs so hard he cries.
> (Grade 10 boy, New Brunswick)

> Our teachers get mad and upset awful quick therefore many students are not on the up and up with them, no talking, no laughing... teacher is prejudice against you.
> (Grade 11 boy, Newfoundland and Labrador)

Some teachers treat you really hard, and they are always picking
on you, even if it's not fault. Some of the teachers like to
embarrass you all the time. How can school be fun like this?
(Grade 10 girl, Newfoundland and Labrador)

School is boring.... It seems like some teachers pick a person
to pick on all the time and a person to be their pet.
(Grade 11 girl, Prince Edward Island)

Teachers take the fun out of school. One of them picks on
certain kids in the class which is unfair and he is always down
on the females, especially two certain ones.
(Grade 9 girl, Nova Scotia)

I think I don't like is that one of the teachers at this school picks
on me just because I wear an earring in my left ear.
(Grade 9 boy, Nova Scotia)

After complaining she did not enjoy school to the extent that she would like, a

Grade 9 girl in Nova Scotia wrote: "People who are intelligent cannot enjoy school, because

they have people putting them down all the time". She may have been referring to teachers

or students, or both.

Equal Treatment

It is not surprising to find students suggesting that all students should be

treated equally in the school. As stated by one Grade 10 Nova Scotia girl, "Everyone should

have and equal chance, but not too much freedom." As illustrated below, equal treatment

means for some students that teachers should have a sense of humour with all students, or

with none of them:

I feel that everybody should be treated the same way no certain
people should be treated different. Not laughing with some and
serious with the rest.
(Grade 9 girl, Nova Scotia)

112

Teachers should put more humour in their teaching. They
should put away their personal attitudes towards some students
they dislike and treat everyone equal.
(Grade 10 girl, Nova Scotia)

While arguments for recognizing individual differences among students may

point to the need for different interaction strategies when dealing with different students, the

universal nature (within the classroom) of a sense of humour has been alluded to:

All people are created equal but not identical. They must be
taught as individuals and not as faceless statistics. Teachers
should smile more often and everyone should have an equal
chance, but not too much freedom.
(Grade 9 boy, Nova Scotia)

Sarcastic and Insulting Teachers

On some occasions, teachers' remarks which students felt were intended "to be

funny" or "just a joke" have been interpreted by them as "sarcastic", "insulting", or

"humiliating". After observing that some of her "teachers think they are funny", a Grade 11

girl in New Brunswick complained: "Many teachers are too sarcastic." She continued by

asking: "Why should we respect them when they don't even respect us?" In a similar vein, a

Grade 11 boy in a different New Brunswick school wrote:

Many of the teachers in this school are sarcastic, unreasonable,
are living in the past, and do not respect your opinion.

Other students' observations which suggest that some high school teachers, at

least on certain occasions, are sarcastic and insulting to their students, rather promoting a

positive sense of humour in teacher-student interactions include the following:

Teachers... are sarcastic and don't like to listen to students'
opinions. If they listened to us they would realize their
smartness is not funny. But this is just some teachers. Overall

113

I enjoy coming to school and being with the people.
(Grade 11 girl, New Brunswick)

Some of the my teachers are too sarcastic and do not give a care
about the students. They laugh at you all the time.
(Grade 11 boy, Nova Scotia)

My teachers, well, some of them are really mean with their
jokes, some of them even insult the students
(Grade 10 girl, Nova Scotia)

I, myself, think that teachers should not be aloud to criticize the
students or call them names to embarrass them. They think it is
fun.
(Grade 9 girl, Nova Scotia)

There are certain teachers in this school who do not treat
students fairly. One in particular seems to enjoy insulting some
of the students.
(Grade 11 girl, Newfoundland and Labrador)

Teachers are too insulting, and some teachers make fun of their
students.
(Grade 10 boy, Newfoundland and Labrador)

One can imagine the role that student-perceived reactions of their classmates

play in the development of their emotions in responding to teachers "insults". Students have

been known to be empathetic to each other's plight under such circumstances:

There are certain teachers in this school who do not treat
students fairly. One in particular seems to enjoy insulting some
of the students. This makes the student involved bitter and also
his fellow classmates
(Grade 11 girl, Newfoundland and Labrador)

They have also reported to have been further insulted and humiliated by the reactions of their

classmates to a teacher's sardonic actions:

114

> I hate the way the science teacher makes me feel right shitty and
> everything by saying things about me, and all the people in the
> class laughs at you and starts teasing you about it.
> (Grade 9 boy, Newfoundland and Labrador)

The significance of others to high school students as they react to what they

perceive to be negative teaching techniques can be further illustrated with students' comments

that include references to their being "in front of the class" (see below) when such strategies

are directed at them.

Making Fun of Students

An earlier analysis of students' observations has revealed that several students

in three of the four Atlantic provinces claimed that some of their teachers "make fun of"

them (Martin, 1985b: 51-53; 1987). For example, translating the comments of one Grade 9

Francophone New Brunswick boy one gets this opinion:

> There are some teachers, who I think, like to make fun of the
> students if they're having problems, like Mr._____. He has
> often made fun of me and of a lot of my friends as well. He's
> is one of the few teachers I don't like.

The comment of a Grade 10 student in Prince Edward Island suggests that teachers pick on

certain students each day and make "smart jokes at" their expense. She wrote:

> "A few teachers try to embarrass you by making smart jokes at
> your expense and by just picking on you."

As implied in some students' claims that teachers make fun of them in the

presence of other students, teachers derive a certain amount of pleasure from such an

exercise. Other students look at teachers' actions as a misguided teaching strategy.

Whatever the objective reality of the situation, the fact that such actions are taken when

students are "in front of the class" is of critical significance to many. Other points of

115

interest in students comments relating to how they view their teachers' making fun of them include teachers' references to clothing, private matters, and incorrect answers. First, examples will be given of students observations on teachers who make fun of them in front of the class.

In Front of the Class

While student comments often suggest significant others are present when teachers insult and humiliate their students, thereby making it more difficult for them to deal with such negativism from a teacher, a number of students (responding to the present request for them to share their concerns about schooling with the researchers) made explicit reference to being "in front of the class" when the teacher embarrassed, insulted or humiliated them:

> ... at times though I feel that the teachers do not respect the students sense of pride and many times attempt to humiliate people in front of their fellow students.
> (Grade 11 girl, Nova Scotia)

> I haven't been making very good marks since I entered Junior High. I find the work difficult and I find if you ask a teacher for help, they could joke about it. They aren't too concerned or they embarrass you in front of the class.
> (Grade 9 girl, Nova Scotia)

> There are teachers that will sit and rap with you all day. Others just seem to be here for the money. They won't help you and usually try to get smart with you. They do this to try to embarrass you in front of others when you ask a question.
> (Grade 11 boy, Nova Scotia)

> Teachers also tend to embarrass students in front of the rest of the class. I don't think this is funny.
> (Grade 10 girl, Newfoundland and Labrador)

... I also think some teachers embarrass students by either
picking on or criticizing them in front of the class. When they
are laughed at, the pupils get discouraged.
(Grade 10 girl, Newfoundland and Labrador)

Teachers in this school don't like me at all. I can feel their
dislike when they talk to me in the classroom. They crack jokes
about me in front of my friends,....
(Grade 11 girl, Newfoundland and Labrador)

I agree that students may need scolding now and then for certain
actions they may have done, or for not doing an assignment,
however, no student needs to be picked out of a crowd and
ridiculed and made fun of in front of a whole class, sometimes
for the whole period.
(Grade 12 girl, New Brunswick)

This is a good school. But one problem I find in my school is
the principal. He's always mouthing off and acting tough guy
all the time. He likes to make fun of and embarrass a student in
front of others just to look big.
(Grade 10 boy, New Brunswick)

Without noting the presence of others, students have complained that teachers

sometimes make fun of particular dimensions of a student's appearance, academic

performance and/or behaviour. More specifically, students participating in the present

research complained about teachers' reference to their clothing, highlighting their "wrong

answers" and interfering with their "private matters".

Incorrect Answers

The satisfaction of Newfoundland and Labrador students with the help they get

from teachers when they give incorrect answers to teachers' questions (when they make

mistakes) and when they seek help from their teachers has been discussed elsewhere (Martin,

1983:34-36). On the other hand, the causes of embarrassment among high school students in

Atlantic Canada have been shown to include teachers' reactions to students who give

117

incorrect answers to their questions (Martin, 1985b:41-45; 1985c:40-44). While such

reactions are not always intended to be humorous, students sometimes think teachers are

"trying to be funny" in their responses to students' mistakes.

Here is a sample of students' comments which suggest their displeasure with

teachers whom they accuse of making fun of their incorrect answers:

> ...also, I don't like teachers who pick on students or make fun
> of them if they get a wrong answer.
> (Grade 10, Prince Edward Island)

> It makes me mad when I can't go up and ask a teacher to help
> me without them bawling my head off for not knowing it.
> (Grade 9 girl, New Brunswick)

> The actions of certain teachers bother me... humiliating you...
> because of a test you have written in the past and making fun of
> your mark.
> (Grade 9 girl, New Brunswick)

> A lot of the teachers expect too much from you. Some tell you
> the work to do, give you one example and expect you to do it
> right with no other help. Some enjoy embarrassing students in
> front of a class by reading off you marks if you do bad or
> making a sarcastic comment.
> (Grade ...., New Brunswick)

> When a teacher asked a student a question and that student gets
> it wrong they laugh at him, and then he (the student) feels bad.
> (Grade 9 boy, Newfoundland and Labrador)

> A teacher says if you want help come up and get it and then if
> you can't answer it she will yell and scream at you and make
> you feel embarrassed. ...sometimes others are laughing at you.
> (Grade 9 girl, Nova Scotia)

Clothing

While it is not one of the more salient issues in schooling, the fact that

teachers are sometimes perceived as making fun of what students wear to school is obviously

118

important to some students. For example, a Grade 10 girl in New Brunswick pointed to the question of whether or not certain students can afford to dress like others. She also wondered what teachers reactions would be if students openly made fun of what they wore:

> Also, I feel the teachers shouldn't say anything about what we wear to school. Maybe some students can only afford so much, compared to others. Matter of fact it's true not every kid can afford fancy clothes. I just wonder what the teacher would do if we said we don't like what he has on? I wonder what he would do if we made fun of his clothes in class.

Another New Brunswick girl, this one in Grade 12, claimed that it was the female teachers who "make fun of and talk too much about the way the young people dress". She also expressed the view that teachers do not behave in this way toward their pets. A third New Brunswick girl, in another school, claimed to be speaking on behalf of others rather then herself when she wrote:

> I have never had any really bad experiences with teachers in this school but I know of people who have and which bothers me because of actions of the teachers. Such as humiliating you by making fun of what you are wearing, ...

Rather than identifying teachers as the culprits in making fun of their clothes, some students expressed their annoyance with being the butt of jokes from other students who laugh at the way they are dressed. To quote a Grade 10 New Brunswick girl:

> My main concern is students laughing at other students because of their clothes or whatever. I feel that if you are a student which is being laughed at it ruins your schooling experience.

Private Matters

Aside from one's clothes, as already described, a plethora of issues such as boyfriend/girlfriend relationships while in the school and what students do while away from

119

the school but seen by some to interfere with their school lives may be considered as private

matters by different students. The association between teachers' bringing "private matters",

which relate to student identity, action and plan of action, as defined by students, into the

public domain of the classroom and the occurrence of student embarrassment has been

illustrated in Martin (1985b:49-51; 1985c:48). Focusing specifically on private matters and

humour, a Grade 9 girl in New Brunswick wrote:

> ...touching on private matters really upsets me, and really these
> things shouldn't be discussed in the classroom. It's not fair to
> make jokes of private matters.

A second Grade 9 New Brunswick girl in a different school reported:

> Another thing that bothers me is when teachers make you feel
> embarrassed in school by asking you stupid questions that are
> personal. I hate it when teachers start putting down and
> laughing at things you like to do.

Moods

As identified by high school students in Atlantic Canada, both the teachers'

moods and the moods of the students influence the extent and nature of humour in the

classroom.

Teachers' Moods

Many students placed their teachers into contrasting groups with respect to

their moods. To illustrate, here are some of their comments:

> I like some of my teachers because they are good heads but
> most of my teachers are grouches and very boring.
> (Grade 11 girl, New Brunswick)

> Some of the teachers can be real crabs when they want to be,
> but most of them are all right.
> (Grade 10 girl, New Brunswick)

As far as the teachers concern goes, on the whole is very good.
There are real crabs, and then there are those who are really
concerned.
(Grade 11 girl, New Brunswick)

Some teachers are nice and some can be really ignorant.
(Grade 10 girl, Prince Edward Island)

They (teachers) are usually very helpful and cooperative but
sometimes let their moods get in the way of teaching.
(Grade 12, girl, New Brunswick)

Some teachers are nice some not and they all are quite moody.
(Grade 12 girl, Nova Scotia)

Most of the teachers here are reasonable, but some of them can
be irritable at times.
(Grade 12 girl, Nova scotia)

According to students there are several causes of changes in teachers' mood.

One such cause is "domestic problems or problems of other kinds" that "should be left where

they belong not brought to the job" (Grade 9 Newfoundland girl). Comments from students

in each of four provinces were in line with that of one Grade 11 girl in New Brunswick who

observed that teachers sometimes "come to school in a rotten mood and they take all their

anger out on students." In school factors have also been identified as a source of teachers'

moodiness. Some students noted that they themselves may be the culprit in the situation.

For example, after remarking that "some teachers are very cranky at times", a Grade 11 girl

in Prince Edward Island added: "I guess they a have a right to be at times, but not all the

time." The comments of a Grade 9 girl in Nova Scotia is another example of the view that

students are the reasons why teachers become "cranky". She wrote that teachers "can be

very cranky to students but in order for them to be cranky the student usually causes s/he to be that way." One Grade 9 Nova Scotia boy argued: "Just because one class spoiled their mood doesn't mean they have to take it out on another."

Among the consequences of teachers' "bad moods" as reported by students are teachers' "hollering" and "yelling" at students, and even "kicking" them out the classroom. In the words of a Grade 10 girl in New Brunswick: "What I don't like is that on a teachers' bad day, they vent their problems on the students." More specific to the topic of classroom humour, here are observations which suggest an association between teachers' moods and this dimension of teacher-student interaction:

> Sometimes the teachers are in a bad mood and take it out students by hollering at them, kicking them out of class. Sometimes the classes are boring because the teacher doesn't put life in it, being to serious. They never smile, joke when in a bad mood.
> (Grade 10 boy, Nova Scotia)

> I find that teachers can be very repulsive if they start the morning terrible. They yell for no reason. They are cranky for the whole day. No fun, no joking around all serious for the day. If you come in the door the wrong way they'll yell that you slammed the door.
> (Grade 11 girl, New Brunswick)

> Some teachers may have a problem at home, which puts them in a bad mood, but the worse thing about it is that they bring this mood to school, and take their bad times out on the students, which is not fair. We cannot joke of laugh.
> (Grade 11 girl, New Brunswick)

> I find some teachers in this school to be quite short tempered, they can joke around for awhile then all of a sudden can a get very angry. I find this puzzling.
> (Grade 12 girl, New Brunswick)

I wish that they would change some of the teachers, because they don't know how to explain things to the students, and some of them are always in a bad mood and make fun of us.
(Grade 11 girl, New Brunswick -- translated from French)

... and some days the teachers may be cross at you for no reason and that spoils the whole day. You can't crack smile. On other days they are in extremely good moods.
(Grade 9 boy, Nova Scotia)

Students' Moods

While a Grade 11 boy in New Brunswick claimed that "teachers are ok, but they are usually on the bad side of a mood, not like the students happy and fun going", students representing a number of schools in each of the four Atlantic provinces reported that students, as well as teachers, have their "bad days". To quote from one student in each province,

Naturally, every student has bad days when he is not in the mood to work, whether because he is discouraged or because he is tired.
(Grade 12 girl, New Brunswick -- translated from French)

I usually like school but sometimes I get in certain moods like the one I'm in now. A state of depression.
(Nova Scotia, Grade 9 boy)

Our teachers never lets us do anything because they're to crooked. I am crooked too.
(Grade 9 boy, Newfoundland)

... some of the staff are also grumpy, so why can't we be grumpy?
(Grade 9 boy, Prince Edward Island)

Different students echoed the comments of the Grade 11 girl in Nova Scotia who reported that if teachers "have a bad day, the students have to put up with it, but if we have a bad one, they jump all over us" and those of the Grade 11 girl in New Brunswick

123

who suggested that "teachers should be considerate to students who are having a 'bad day' and leave them alone". While this may be a legitimate suggestion for some situations, it may also be that students' bad moods are sometimes associated with their own actions, which they may perceive to be humorous but which their teachers define as disruptive behaviour and not conducive to a positive classroom environment.

PART III

CLASSROOM OBSERVATIONS

The context and forms of classroom humour are illustrated in this part of our study of the schooling experiences of high school students in Atlantic Canada. Through episodes of humour, identified from observations and interviews, the context of classroom humour is shown to include: (1) institutional characteristics relating to family background, mass media, sports, sex-role stereotyping and politics; (2) organizational dimensions of teacher authority and expertise, class time and school environment; (3) formal curriculum with particular reference to history, literature, science, mathematics and religion; and (4) teacher and student identities. The classroom humour described often takes the form of the ambiguity of words as illustrated by puns, homonyms, misunderstandings and playing with names. Other forms of classroom humour identified in the present research are sarcasm, student wit, story telling, impersonations and practical jokes. While humour expressed in any one of these forms may also employ features of body language, nonverbal actions have been pinpointed here as a particular form of classroom humour.

CHAPTER 7

CONTEXT OF CLASSROOM HUMOUR

There are overlapping and intertwining institutional, organizational and curriculum domains, on the one hand, and self and group processes, on the other, that may be seen as constituting the social context of classroom humour. Drawing on a variety of episodes of such humour, the present chapter illustrates the institutional, organizational and curriculum contexts of classroom humour, and reveals the subtleties of self and group processes which anchor the meaning of this humour within the realities of the classroom. It should be emphasized that the idea of separating the social context of classroom humour into four parts (institutional, organizational, curriculum and self/group processes) is for clarity of presentation only. While the influence of a specific dimension of the social context may be seen to be greater in one any example of classroom humour, any one episode of humour may be used to in fact illustrate the influence of more than one dimension of the social context as envisaged here.

Institutional Context

In order to capture the different dimensions of the school-society dichotomy as suggested by various examples of classroom humour, the present discussion assigns two separate meanings to the idea of institutional context of classroom humour. Institutional context refers, first, to the classroom, school, community, province, country and global community as institutional frameworks. The second meaning is in line with the more

127

conventional anthropological use of the term "institutions", that is, in reference to religion, kinship, politics, economy and mass media as examples of institutions.

With respect to the institutional entities of classroom, school, community and so on, the social context of classroom humour is relatively easy to identify. In one conceptual framework the classroom is seen as the smallest of a number of concentric circles, and one proceeds by moving outward from the classroom which exists in the context of the school, and from the school which exists in the context of a neighbourhood or community, and so to a region, a province, a country and the global community. Another more meaningful framework, as illustrated by different examples of classroom humour, depicts each of these institutional entities as having direct linkages to the classroom. By way of categorizing classroom humour that appears to reflect the institutional context of the classroom, four overlapping groupings have been identified here, consisting of family background, mass media, sports, sex-role stereotyping and politics.

Family Background

A student's family background is often an important factor in students' classroom life because it is brought into the classroom in many ways, some more overt than others. One teacher's complaint about one of his students as presented in the situation "You Are Just Like Your Brother" is one way the kinship institution becomes part of classroom realities.

You Are Just Like Your Brother

Setting
A Grade 11 classroom where the Biology teacher, Mr. A, was having difficulty in classroom management. Despite Mr. A's repeated instructions to the class in general, and to specific

128

students, for them to get back to their seats, to get their biology books out, and to stop talking to each other, several students continued to misbehave.

Student
Felix, one of the boys in the class, was from the teacher's perspective especially hard to control. Felix's brother is in another of the teacher's classes, and is seen among teachers to be often "causing problems" for them.

Episode
After repeatedly attempting to get Felix to be less disruptive and to be more attentive, Mr. A walked toward Felix and angrily said that he was just like his brother. While two of the nearby students appeared to think this was funny, Felix was seemingly oblivious to Mr. A's remarks. After the teacher moved away from Felix, those two students jokingly referred to Felix by his brother's name. Felix was not amused.

Mass Media

The mass media are another societal institution that has a major influence on classroom humour. Here is an obvious example of how a teacher's television viewing enters into the life of the classroom.

A Television Joke

Setting
The teacher was highlighting the materials which he wanted his Grade 11 students to review as they prepared for a unit test in mathematics.

Episode
Without any reference to the mathematics lesson, the teacher asked if anyone had seen the Johnny Carson show on Television the previous evening. Nobody indicated he/she had seen it and the teacher proceeded to tell a joke that he had heard on the show. Before the teacher had completed the joke, a student interrupted and asked if "it", in reference to the joke, "is going to be on the tests". Immediately, almost the entire class burst into laughter. After the laughter subsided, the teacher continued with the joke he had heard on television.

129

Results

As evidenced by the comments and smiles directed toward the student who had asked if the joke was to be on the test, his inquiry, rather than the story which the teacher relayed from a television show, became the focal point of the humour for the students in this situation.

Sports

The significant influence of the mass media is obvious in the episodes of classroom humour given here as examples of the role sports play in such humour. Sports is identified as a separate category because it is likely that local sports can be the subject of joking remarks in this setting, though no such remarks were heard in the present classroom observations.

Too Bad the Canadians Are Not Playing Better

Background

The teacher knew that there were some staunch Montreal Canadians' hockey fans in his class. The Canadians were not doing as well as their fans would have liked.

Episode

After the bell had rung for the class to begin, but prior to getting into the formal curriculum, a teacher jokingly remarked that it was too bad that the Canadians were not playing better. The humour did not stop with the teacher's comment as a couple of the students became defensive to the teacher and to other students who teased them about the "weaknesses" of the Montreal Canadians hockey team.

A Sudden Diversion

While in the midst of a lesson, and for no apparent reason, one teacher asked if anyone had heard the morning sports news. He said that he had not heard the news, and he wanted to know if the Blue Jays were still in first place. There were chuckles among the students who reported that the Jays were still in first place. Knowing that the teacher was not a Blue Jay fan, one

boy laughed as he commented that they would remain on top for
the rest of the season.

Sex-Role Stereotyping

It is well known that sex-role stereotyping has been a part of classroom culture

since the beginning of schooling. The extent to which such processes are created within the

classroom itself or are a mere reflection of the broader societal context in contemporary

society is an empirical question. Despite the reduction of sex-role stereotyping in textbooks

in recent years and the attention given to breaking down sex-role stereotyping in interactions

of everyday life, it is obvious that stereotyping is still a part of the classroom humour in

some schools. As seen in the following examples, this type of stereotyping is implied in a

variety of classroom settings and on a range of substantive topics.

Absenteeism

One male teacher was heard questioning why so many girls
were often absent from classes. His suggestion that certain girls
are always sick brought a few smiles and chuckles from a
couple of the boys present.

Hockey Equipment

The issue of female participation in sports was discussed during
a gathering of students at a volleyball game in the school
gymnasium. One of them questioned why girls did not play
hockey. In obvious reference to differences in body shape
between male and females, one boy commented that girls would
not need as much equipment as boys. Another boy jokingly
remarked that they would not need a jock strap while another
added they would need less padding as well.

A Broken Leg

A girl, who had sprained her ankle, spent several days walking
with the assistance of crutches. One morning, before classes
started, a male teacher was overheard asking her how her leg

was. Some of the boys who were present at the time seemed to imply that the teacher's question was not appropriate as they attempted to create humour at the expense of the teacher. Before the girl with the crutches responded one boy, in a loud voice, exclaimed: "Sir!" "Oh, did you hear that?" asked another boy immediately. A third fellow followed with: "Get his question?" Other students, both male and female, were laughing and talking as those students made verbal responses to the teacher's original inquiry about the girl's leg.

Joe Should Be A Cheerleader

Background
Arrangements had been made for the school cheerleaders to meet in the gymnasium ten minutes before formal classes were over for the day.

Setting
As the time of the cheerleader meeting arrived, a Level III girl reminded her teacher, Mr. Brown, that she and others in the class were to attend a meeting in the gymnasium. Mr. Brown quickly reviewed the plans for the next class before giving the cheerleaders permission to attend their meeting.

Episode
While four of the approximately twelve girls present were leaving the classroom, Mr. Brown asked if any of the boys were going to the cheerleaders' meeting. In response to this query, there was laughter in the classroom and several boys made comments to one another. For example, one boy jokingly asked another why he did not become a cheerleader. A second fellow, in specific reference to a boy in the room, said: "Joe should go with the girls."

Despite Mr. Brown's immediate attempt to restore order to his class, two or three minutes had passed before the teacher-student interaction resembled that which had existed prior to his query about whether any of the boys were going to the cheerleaders meeting.

The Bottom Line

Setting
A classroom where 25 high school students were discussing the potential for the development of new business ventures, entrepreneurial skills and good business practices.

Episode
One of the students, Jean, who was sometimes admired for her figure, got up from her seat to leave the classroom at a moment when a topic relating to balancing the books was being discussed. Bob, another student in the classroom, in an apparent reference to Jean's body shape (he was smiling and looking at her as she was leaving the room), said: "The bottom line is what counts." A small number of students lightheartedly smiled and one of them scornfully observed, "That's not funny." The teacher continued with the discussion not realizing (pretending not to realize?) the reference to Jean's physical appearance.

Your Name Is Not Trina

Setting
Level I mathematics class with 25 students present.

Teaching Method
Teacher is "reviewing" and "correcting" mathematics problems that were assigned during the previous mathematics class. She was identifying individual students to give answers to specific problems and to explain how he/she arrived at the answer. If a student's answer was incorrect, the teacher asked for an explanation of how the student arrived at the answer.

Episode
The teacher asked: "Trina, how did you factor number 7 on page 72?"
Chris, immediately responded, "The y's cancel out, Miss, and ..."
The teacher interrupted: "Chris, your name is not Trina."
Another student quickly responded: "Oh yes, it is, Miss."

Class Response
With few exceptions, the students broke into loud laughter and turned their attention to Chris. Even the teacher paused and

smiled before proceeding with the task at hand. As she
redirected her question to Trina, several students were looking
at Chris and referring to him as Trina. Two of them continued
to address Chris in this way for the remainder of the
mathematics correcting exercise which was about ten minutes.
In fact, this behaviour continued, albeit with less frequency,
throughout the remainder of the 45 minute class period.

Broader Context
Follow up observations of, and discussions with, students in this
class revealed that many of Chris's classmates saw him as one
who spent an unusual amount of time associating with the
females in his class, and he was the target in other joking
relations relating to his associations with the girls in his class.

Politics

Sociologically, the idea of politics includes a wide gamut of processes and
structures from the small group to societal and global social organizations. For example, the
influence of the mass media on classroom humour and the process of sex-role stereotyping as
exemplified in classroom humour are not separate from the politics of contemporary society.
The present focus on politics as a separate category in the institutional context of classroom
humour selects situations where politicians and political parties are introduced as subjects for
classroom humour.

The comments of one teacher that the premier of the province should be in the
province dealing with provincial matters rather than on vacation in the sun brought smiles of
approval from students in his class. Another teacher's suggestion that a particular politician,
who had been defeated in the elections, should be put to rest with a senate appointment was
considered funny by many of the students in a Grade 12 social studies class. As reported by
teachers and students, there was one student in their school they jokingly referred to as a

134

politician. Apparently, he got this label because of his verbosity on whatever topic was brought up both within and outside the classroom.

A teacher's suggestion that there were too many parties in the federal election brought smiles and joking remarks about some of the "fringe parties" and their leaders.

Too Many Parties

Background
The country was in the midst of a federal election campaign with a record number of political parties participating. Issues relating to the number of political parties were receiving attention in the media. The level I class where this observation was made spent considerable time discussing the election. The back wall of the classroom was decorated with newspaper clippings on the election.

Episode
The teacher suggested that there were too many parties participating in the federal election. His reasons included the view that there are too many parties to keep track of and it would be difficult to get a majority government.

This suggestion met with the approval of many of the students present as they joined in with joking remarks about the leaders of, what they perceived to be, "fringe parties". Their comments and questions included: "Who is (party leader's name) anyhow?" "Where does he come from?" "Did you see him last night (on television)"? "He must be crazy."

Organizational Context

At least two dimensions of the organizational domain of the classroom and school become important elements in classroom humour. One is the rules and regulations that are designed to control the behaviour of students and, to a lesser extent, of teachers. The other is the status difference between teacher and students as grounded in curriculum knowledge and teaching strategies. These dimensions of the organizational context get worked out in the school, to a large extent, through the negotiation of teacher and student identities in the classroom setting. Detailed examples of these identities are given later in this chapter. Observations of classroom humour that relate to the issue of teacher authority and teacher expertise are presented here.

Teacher Authority

While issues relating to the authority of the teacher in the classroom have been of interest to researchers and practitioners for decades, it has recently come to occupy an even more dominant place in the study and practice of schooling. In addition to the question of authoritarian versus democratic modes of control, a contemporary concern is the extent to which schools have lost control of, and can exert any meaningful control over, student behaviour that is disruptive of teaching and learning. While not dealing with serious cases of disruptive behaviours, the following examples of teacher-student interactions indicate the presence of humour, at least from the perspective of some students, in situations where the teacher is attempting to control student behaviour.

A Loud Outburst

A teacher was experiencing difficultly in getting some of her students to pay more attention to her while she was talking. She made repeated requests to the class in general and gave directives to specific students to "be quiet", to "get your books out" and to "listen". At one point she seemingly lost control of herself and loudly instructed Jonathan to move from the seat he was in at the back of the classroom to occupy one at the front of the class. Immediately, some students made light of this situation as they laughed and jokingly repeated the teacher's instruction for Jonathan to move to the front of the room.

136

T-Shirt

Background
A Grade 9 girl who had a reputation for wearing "different" and
sometimes "odd" clothing to school. On the day this
observation was made she wore was an unusually decorated T-
shirt that was obviously much larger than was normally worn
by people her size.

Joking Relationships
Although not observed by the researcher, student reports were
that they "made fun" of this girl's T-shirt at different times
during the day. While some thought it was "cool," others were
not so positive in their comments on it.

Final Episode
As the last class of the day was about to end, Ms. B. looked at
the girl with the oversized and decorated T-shirt and
commanded: "Do not come in class with that shirt on
tomorrow." Different students smiled as they looked at this
student, who seemed to enjoy the attention from teacher and
students.

Mr. Who?

A teacher threatened that if Blanche continued to misbehave he
would send her to Mr. D's (the principal's) office.
"Mr who?" replied Blanche to this warning, much to the joy of
a small number of students in her class.

It Is only Nick

A substitute teacher was in the classroom as the students
arrived. While some of them asked why he was there, others
stated the question differently and asked why the regular teacher
was absent.
One student appeared to be surprised as he entered the
classroom to find the substitute, as he was overheard
commenting to a fellow student that "we only have Nick" today.
Obviously some of the students who heard this comment thought
it was funny.
Note

The substitute teacher's name was Nicholas. It was unusual for
students to refer to a teacher or a substitute teacher by his/her
first name, especially a shortened version of his/her name.

Teacher Expertise

Given the status differences in the classroom with teachers as experts in formal

knowledge relating to the school curriculum and teacher strategies, it is not surprising that

humour may arise, especially from the student perspective, when a teacher's expertise is

open to question. As seen in the "Troublesome Words" example, a teacher's mistake may in

itself produce amusement and laughter among students. However, there are indications that

a teacher's reaction after the mistake, rather than the mistake itself, is often the core element

of the humour. When a teacher is perceived as pretending that he/she has not made a

mistake, in other words that what was said was intentional, students become suspicious of the

teacher's claim and the pretence becomes the joke among the students.

A Mistake?

A teacher was writing Algebraic equations on the blackboard as
he was explaining them. At one point he put incorrect
information on the board, but he continued as if everything he
had written was correct. One student alertly pointed out the
inaccuracy. The teacher immediately acknowledged the problem
and claimed that it was intentional on his part to see if anyone
would recognize that it was inaccurate. Several students
laughed and later told the researcher that they thought the
inaccuracy was a mistake. It was not intentional. This teacher,
from the student perspective, had made other "mistakes" earlier
in the year, which contributed to the student-perceived humour
in the present situation.

Troublesome Words

A teacher returned students' essays to them at the beginning of
an English class. While grading the essays the teacher had
corrected the spelling mistakes in each essay. She had made a

138

list of the words that were incorrectly spelt with the intent of
sharing this list of "troublesome words" with the class. During
the class she proceeded to write each of these words on the
blackboard while she talked about the pronunciation of each
word and why each may present some difficulty to students.
Joe, a student, had spelled "scene" incorrectly ("scence"). The
teacher had made the necessary correction in his essay and
added a side note to the student that read "one 'c'". However,
much to the pleasure of Joe, the teacher wrote "scence" on the
blackboard. When Joe brought the teacher's mistake to his
attention other students appreciated the humour of the situation,
at the teacher's expense.
Over the next week or so, the teacher was reminded of this
"one c" episode.

The social structure of the classroom as reflected in teacher expertise versus

student lack of knowledge is demonstrably a significant element in the development of

different episodes of school humour reported on in the "curriculum context" section below.

Class Time

Another aspect of the organization of the classroom which seems to play an

significant role in the development of classroom humour is the structuring of class time. A

considerable portion of classroom humour occurs both prior to the start of the class while the

students are gathering or are assembled in the room and during the early part of the lesson.

She's here, Miss

While the teacher was taking attendance at the beginning of a
class Jo Ann, who was apparently engrossed in something, did
not respond to her name. After the teacher repeated Jo Ann's
name, a student who was sitting close to Ann replied, in a loud
and clear voice: "She's here, Miss." Jo Ann was quickly
alerted as students' laughed at her friend's reply to the teacher.

139

Wake-up Call

Background
Mr. Jones, a history teacher, had a reputation among his students as a "boring teacher". They claimed that he rigidly adhered to the textbook, his tone of voice rarely changed and he often used "big words". Hence, for many students, his classes were very monotonous.

Setting
The class had come to order, Mr. Jones had made reference to the material which had been covered during their last history class, and had noted the readings which the students were expected to have studied in preparation for the day's class.

Episode
He was about to start a lecture on the assigned reading when Peter, a student seated round the middle of the classroom, looked at the person sitting on one side of him and asked, in a voice that was heard throughout the room: "Give me a wake up call at 11:55".

Student Responses
Immediately, almost the entire class broke into loud and seemingly uncontrollable laughter. A few students were more restrained as they light heartedly laughed and/or smiled.

Teacher Response
At first, the Mr. Jones appeared to be upset with Peter's "intrusion", as he looked stern faced at him. Then, he briefly smiled as he moved to one side of the classroom. While returning to his desk at the front of the room, Mr. Jones attempted to focus the class on the assigned reading. However, the laughing, giggling and talking continued, albeit at a reduced level. Shortly thereafter, Mr. Jones told the class that all of them needed a "wake up" call. He then proceeded to lecture on the importance of paying attention while in class, on the necessity of studying the assigned materials before the class begins, and on the need for commitment to school work if students are to do anything with their lives.

School Environment

Both teachers and students have been known to joke about one or another aspect of the school environment outside of the classroom. And on occasion, they display such negative meanings for some dimension of this organization. For example, one teacher received the approval of his students when he questioned the need for so many rules for student behaviour in the school corridors. They chuckled when he observed that senior high students should have more freedom than they are given in his school. Similarly, students and teachers were of one accord in the "Cafeteria Food" example given below.

Cafeteria Food

The teacher called her class to order and instructed the students to get their books out in preparation for the Literature period which was about to begin. Many of the students were talking to one another in a normal tone of voice, though much of their conversation was not understood by the observer. However, one student was heard to remark that the chips she had for lunch in the school cafeteria were not very good. Another student jokingly added that "none of the stuff" they had in the cafeteria was any good. The conversation about the cafeteria food continued until the class had started, with a third student claiming that "it is not fit to eat". Even the teacher joked about the blandness of the cafeteria food.

Curriculum Context

While there may be a particular mix of a wide range of variables (e.g., which teachers and students are present at the time, previous experiences of the actors with each other, classroom climate) in the humour found at any one time in the classroom, the formal curriculum topic at a specific point in time was a critical component in the development of some episodes of classroom humour. In fact, it is obvious that the following episodes in

141

History, Literature, Science, Mathematics and Religion would not have occurred in the absence of the particular topic being discussed.

History

Two examples where topics within history lesson became an integral part of the humour are "Napoleon's Age" and "His story".

Napoleon's Age

During a class discussion about people who have played major roles in world history, one student wondered what the dates of Napoleon Bonapart's life were. Rather than answer this question himself, the teacher directed it to the class.
One student responded that Napoleon lived in both the 18th and 19th centuries, and another that he was born in 1769.
After several incorrect guesses as to the date of Napoleon's death, the teacher focused the attention of the class on John, a student, who he thought was not paying attention to the subject matter at hand.
"John," the teacher asked, "when did Napoleon die?"
"I don't know," replied John. "I don't know, I didn't even know he was sick."
Immediately, there were a few snickers from a small number of students while others smiled as they looked at John. The teacher became upset and proceeded to "lecture" John about his attempts to "be funny". He repeated his view that his answer was not "funny", and then added that John was not as "smart" as he thought he was.

His Story

Setting
As the teacher was calling the students to order in preparation for a history lesson, Joan questioned the teacher on why "history" was named as such. The teacher immediately responded that it was good question.

Momentary Humour
A male student quickly proclaimed that it is "his story" rather than "her story" because of the importance of men in history. While different students, both male and female, thought that this

fellow's response was funny in that they reacted joyfully to it, whatever humour was seen in the remarks soon dissipated as the teacher and other students noted the importance of women in history.

Immediate Results
Among other things, the question arose of whether women had played a less important role than men in society or whether the prominence of men in "written history" was because it has been written by men. A comment that was made in jest was instrumental in starting a serious discussion.

Literature

Four episodes of classroom humour ("Outer Space", "Dressed in Black", "Do Bill" and "Why Didn't You Paraphrase") are among those that could be used to illustrate how topics within literature and related subjects can become a major dimension of humour. The "Outer Space" episode is presented in Chapter 8 to illustrate a misunderstanding in the communication between student and teacher. It and the "Dressed in Black" episode given here are illustrations of comic relief occurring at different times during one 45 minute class period. In fact, these two episodes also illustrate that sometimes there is a ripple effect to humour in that one episode spawns another. It is suspected that such is the case when teacher and student react favourably to the first incident.

Dressed in Black

Background
There were 15 students in a literature class where the teacher was preparing the students to write short stories. Topics covered during this period included possible settings (time and place) for the stories, plot and character.

Episode
Within ten minutes of the "Outer Space" episode, the class was discussing "character" in short stories. Among the things mentioned were character traits, body features and dress.

143

During this discussion one of the boys detailed how he was
going to have the main character dressed in black. As he was
talking, several of the students smiled. It was obvious to them
that the character might have some resemblance to one boy in
the classroom who often dressed conspicuously in black.

Do Bill

The following example of humour was related to the researcher
by the teacher who was teaching at the time it happened.

A teacher spent an entire 45 minute period introducing William
Shakespeare and his writings. Before he got round to assigning
any work to the class on the subject at hand, the bell went
indicating the class time was over. "Sir," asked one student,
"are we going to do Bill again next time?" Instantly, the class
broke into laughter. It was the first time they and the teacher
heard had Shakespeare referred to as "Bill". Shakespeare was
often jokingly referred to as Bill by many of the students for the
remainder of the year.

Why Didn't You Paraphrase?

Background
As part of an extensive assignment, Level II students in one
literature class were to give oral presentations of 8 to 10
minutes on their analysis of selected novels.

Setting
Approximately 20 students were present as the teacher called the
class to order and reviewed the instructions for the class
presentations. Students were invited to comment on one
another's presentations. While there was no comment from the
class on the first presentation, the teacher made several
observations including both positive reinforcers and suggestions
for improvement.

Episode
Mary, the second student to give an oral presentation to the
class, included a number of relatively long quotations from other
writers in her analysis. About five minutes into her
presentation, the teacher interrupted and asked why she had
included such long quotes from others in her paper. Among his
questions were: "Why didn't you paraphrase?" Mary appeared

144

surprised and indicated that she thought this was an appropriate
way to do the assignment.
During the ensuing discussion between the teacher and Mary,
the teacher focused on one of her long quotations and suggested
that she could put those ideas in her own words. Mary replied
that she could not do that because, in her words, "I don't know
what the ideas are, sir?"
Mary's response brought considerable laughter from the entire
class. Even the teacher laughed lightly at Mary's response.

Follow-Up
It was later learned that the students in this class knew that
Mary had included an unusual number of long excerpts from
different books so that her oral presentation would not be too
short. It was reported that she had joked about this strategy to
different students while she was preparing her assignment.

Science

The "practical joke" episode of classroom humour described in Chapter 8 is an

example of classroom humour that was made possible because of the nature of a geology

assignment. The following episode developed during a science lesson on types of

reproduction.

Miss, Is That Intercourse?

Setting
A 45 minute science period in a classroom with a female teacher
and 19 Level I students (12 boys and 7 girls). The lesson was
on "types of reproduction".

Episode
There was some giggling in the classroom as the teacher
introduced the topic, "types of reproduction". But, she was not
distracted by they giggling. She proceeded to give definitions
and examples of the different types of reproduction. While the
teacher was repeating the difference between sexual and asexual
reproduction, one of the male students snickered as he asked if
sexual reproduction was the same as intercourse. Some of the
girls seemingly tittered as the teacher clearly replied: "Yes, that
is intercourse." She simultaneously wrote "INTERCOURSE"

145

on the board in large upper case letters. The giggling seemed to diminish as this teacher continued with the lesson.

Students often employ humour to distract a teacher and to get the attention of other students. However, as illustrated in "Miss, Is That Intercourse?" such a strategy does not always produce the desired effect.

Mathematics

The study of fractions, a topic in mathematics, gave one student an opportunity to bring his wit to bear on the lesson in one classroom (See "Apple Sauce" episode in Chapter 8).

Religion

The topic at hand in one religion class was obviously an important factor in one teacher's decision to tell a story about creation (See "Then He Created Woman" in story telling section of Chapter 8).

Identities in the Classroom

It is obvious that in addition to the institutional, organizational and formal curriculum dimensions of the social context of classroom humour, there are situational and temporal dimensions to classroom settings with respect to group and self processes that seem to generate humour between teachers and students and among students themselves. Although it is often difficult to pinpoint the identities, interactive roles and agenda that are salient in classroom humour, those aspects of self and group processes are undoubtedly interwoven in much of the humour in the school setting.

Student Identities

Present observations on classroom humour suggest that while teacher and student identities are often intricately interlocked, it is necessary in some situations to examine student identities in relation to fellow students as distinct from their identities in relation to their teachers.

Among the names which high school students have been observed using to refer to different groupings among themselves are "air heads", "brains", "bullies", "cuffers", "dumb", "elites", "farmers", "good students", "goofers", "jerks", "jiggers", "jocks", "middle people", "pets", "punks", "snobs" "tough guys", and "wimps". While the present research did not attempt to identify the extent to which students have so internalized these concepts that they have become a part of their classroom and school identities, it is clear that a considerable amount of humour evolves around these and similar types of groupings among students. Here is one example of humour that took place between two students.

A Room Not Finished

Setting
Several Grade 11 students, including Joe and Bill, were mingling in the classroom after the bell rang indicating that classes were to begin in five minutes. The bell would ring on the hour indicating that classes were to begin. It was learned that Joe and Bill were teasing each other before they came to the classroom, and this behaviour continued into the classroom.

Episode
Joe, pointing to Bill's head, jokingly remarked that Bill had "a room not finished." The suggestion of this remark was Bill was "a little foolish, ... crazy". Rather than appearing to be upset with this evaluation, Bill and Joe continued to laugh and talk with each other. At least one other student noted the remark that Bill had a room not finished, and repeated it in a loud voice so that others would hear it.

147

Teachers often attribute identities to their students. The extent to which students perceive themselves to be fulfilling the identities which teachers have assigned them is an empirical question. Similarly, there is an issue of whether students start out with particular identities or whether they take on these identities because of teachers' definitions for them and subsequent actions toward them.

Laziness is a Disease

The teacher was advising his class on the virtues of studying and making good grades in school. Conversely, he noted the consequences of not doing the assigned work and not being successful in one's school work. Without accusing any individual student of being lazy, the teacher observed that "laziness is like a disease", it is contagious. Students may catch it from each other.

Apparently, Jim, one of the students in this class, had a reputation for his lack of interest in school work and for his laziness in the classroom. This view, combined with the teacher's comparing laziness to a disease, gave rise to joking remarks among the students that they had to stay away from Jim so that they would not be infected.

Slow Learning

The teacher directed a question to Jane whom he knew was not likely have the answer. Jane was silent as she looked at her desk. The teacher repeated the question as many of the students looked at Jane. Jane remained silent when the teacher asked if she had read the assigned material. Several of the student's laughed as Jane reported that she had read it.

Commentary

It was later learned that Jane had probably read the material but did not understand it. It usually took her longer to learn things than it did others in her class. Different students thought it was not fair for the teacher to repeat his question to Jane and highlight her slow learning.

Jane's facial expression suggested a sadness, perhaps an embarrassment, and possibly a negative impact on her self-concept.

148

On occasion, students have been observed questioning teachers' actions toward
them, and in so doing they seem to be countering the perceptions which they perceived
teachers have of them. The episode "Why Do You Ask Me?" is one such situation.

Why Do You Ask Me?

Background
Before starting the lesson for the period, the teacher was
attempting to find out which of his students had participated in
disorderly behaviour that had been reported to have taken place
in gymnasium. While lecturing the entire class on the
importance of behaving properly in all parts of the school, the
teacher asked the students if they had seen what had happened in
the gymnasium.

Episode
"Where were you sitting when the disturbance broke out?" the
teacher asked Joshua.
Pretending to be innocent, Joshua replied, "Why do you ask
me?"
Several of the students smiled, others openly laughed, and some
looked with astonishment at Joshua.

Analysis
The humour in this situation was that it was well known that
Joshua was one of the leaders in the disorderly behaviour in
question. Joshua knew that others, including the teacher, were
aware of his involvement. Yet, he had openly asked the teacher
why he had asked him where he was sitting at the time.

Other examples of classroom humour suggest the complexity of attempting to
pinpoint the identities of students and how students are negotiating those identities in their
relationships with their teachers.

It's Not Lost, But I Don't Know Where It Is

Prior to the beginning of a mathematics class, a student was
noisily moving his books and papers across his desk. The
teacher noticed that the student did not have his mathematics

149

textbook which he was expected to have with him for the class that was about to begin. He told the student to go and get his book, because he would need it during the class. The student, however, did not make any move to go for his book.

"Is your book in your locker?" asked the teacher, looking at the student.

"No, sir," replied the student.

The teacher responded with a number of questions including: "Where is it?", "Do you know where it is?", "Is it lost?"

"Not lost, sir," replied the student, "but I don't know where it is."

There was laughter from different parts of the classroom. However, the teacher did not think the student's response was funny and he proceeded to tell him that he might get lost in the rest of the mathematics classes, if he did not "smarten up".

I Expected Better Work from You

Setting

It was toward the end of a Level II English class and the teacher was returning an assignment to the students. Prior to returning the assignments she made some remarks, a combination of positive and negative evaluations, on the overall quality of the assignments. As she returned individual assignments she sometimes made a comment on each. Among other remarks she said: "Your work is improving," "This is well done" and "I was pleased with your essay." The researcher did not detect any teacher or student humour associated with these remarks.

Episode

"I expected better work from you," the teacher commented as she returned one boy's assignment. The boy did not make any verbal response to the teacher. However, other students reacted with pleasure to it. Some of them smiled as they looked toward him, and one student obviously took great pleasure in asking: "What happened Barry,... how come you didn't do better?" Barry pretended to ignore the gloating and teasing of his fellow students.

There are other dimensions to student identity and the process of classroom humour. To elaborate, students sometimes find comic relief from what they perceive to be an authoritarian classroom setting by treating specific dimensions of the school in a light hearted manner. For example, school and classroom rules have been known to be seen as a "joke" because they are not enforced. On a similar vein, a teacher may be seen as a joke because he/she cannot control the classroom.

Also, students have been observed acting as if particular academic expectations are not to be taken seriously. On occasion, homework is not taken seriously by the students because it is not promptly read and graded by the teacher. Different students, representing a number of schools have indicated that under such circumstances "homework is nothing but a joke." Even though the subject assigned to a class period may be defined as an important one, the class period itself, because of a teacher's behaviour, may become known as a joke among students.

Subjects that are perceived to be easy are seen as a joke relative to the difficulty of other subjects. Such perceptions are obviously related to a number of student and social organizational factors, and a particular subject may be perceived in many different ways by any class of 20 or so students. However, Newfoundland Culture and Religion were two subjects that were often viewed as a joke by Newfoundland high schools students in the present study. In exploring this phenomena through interviews, this study finds that students compared the "joke" course with a "serious" one, and that their examples included contrasting Newfoundland culture with academic mathematics, and religion with biology. Furthermore, examinations that are perceived to be too easy are sometimes seen as a joke.

Teacher Identities

As illustrated with student comments in the "Humorous versus Serious Teachers" section in Chapter 5, students have contrasting views of their teachers with respect to the presence or absence of a sense of humour in their interactions with students. Here is an example of humour given by a teacher who is seen to have a sense of humour.

We Need A Revolving Door

A number of students left the classroom for short periods during the first ten minutes or so of a class. With so many going and coming, the teacher decided he needed to control the situation. He told them that before anyone else left he/she would need his permission. Shortly thereafter, a student requested permission to leave the room. The teacher granted him permission and remarked that this classroom needed a revolving door. As evidenced by their responses, this remark was considered to be funny by many of the students in the class.

Note
During follow-up conversations with the researcher, students reported that this remark was typical of this teacher's sense of humour.

However, teachers' efforts to create a particular type of humour do not always yield the desired results. It is perhaps students' perception of the nature of the teachers' humour or perhaps their perception of the teachers themselves which is the most significant factor determining whether a "joke" intended by the teacher is defined as such by the students. The "It Is A Nice Day" episode is an example of teacher defined humour which fails to elicit the desired response from his students.

It Is A Nice Day

Background
A rain storm raged outside as the students hurried into the school from the school buses parked in the school yard. They proceeded to their respective classrooms and the school day began.

Episode
Shortly afterwards the bell rung but, before the formal lesson began, the teacher was heard to comment, with obvious reference to the weather, that "it is a nice day."

Students' Reactions
It was later learned that some students thought the teacher was trying to be funny with his comment on the weather. However, they did not see any humour in his comment. On the contrary, one student observed that it was typical of the teacher's "stupid jokes".

Drawing Attention

A Level III student was often seen sketching figures: head and shoulder drawings as well as full length portraits. These sketches were cartoon-like characters with comic features added that gave them extraordinary appearances. They were known to have been the centre of attention for different groups of students. The fact was that these sketches often drew considerable laughter from others in the class. It was also reported that his teachers often shared a laugh with students over the sketches produced by this student. However, on some occasions, his teachers, one in particular, became annoyed at his drawings, especially when this teacher perceived that the sketches interfered with his formal school work and distracted others from the regular teaching and learning experiences.

Given Me A Break

Students
John and at least two other students were well known by the history teacher and students alike for their lack of studying assigned materials in history.

Episode
At three different times in one history class, the teacher directed questions to John on the assigned topics. On each occasion, it was obvious that John was not familiar with the assigned readings. After responding that he did not know the answer to the third question, John said: "Miss, give me a break." Other students laughed at John's request for a break. There was more laughter as the teacher responded that she would give him a break, but it would not be the kind that he had in mind.

Something in My Throat

A teacher was seeking responses from individually identified
students as he reviewed the material covered during the previous
three or four classes.
At different times during the class, Norman, one of the students,
appeared to be clearing his throat. He made different
movements such as swallowing, opening his mouth wide, and
frequently coughing. Norman's behaviour first got the attention
of another boy who was sitting on the opposite side of the
classroom. Then others directed their attention to Norman.
Momentarily, the teacher looked at Norman and asked if he was
having problems. Norman replied that he had something in his
throat. However, as others realized Norman was putting on an
act, their views on what he had in his throat were verbally
expressed as "nothing" and "his tongue". Several students
laughed and the noise level in the classroom increased
considerably before the lesson got back on track.
It was noted that the teacher did not ask Norman for his input as
he reviewed the previously covered material.

Unsolved questions

Why was Norman seeking attention? Did he want the teacher to
select him for one of his questions? Was Norman pretending to
have something his throat so the teacher would not ask him to
respond to a question? Was Norman just acting up for no
immediate or obvious reason?

A Studious Front

There is a range of situations whereby students have been
observed pretending to know more about the topic at hand than
they do. For particular groups of students, for example, it is
not uncommon for students to pretend to have studied an
assigned lesson, when in fact they have not even read the
material. Such situations are sometimes seen to be humorous
and have been known to bring laughter from other students
present at the time.
During one English class a student who responded, in
considerable details, to his teacher's question about the themes
in one of the short stories assigned to the class to study was
accused by the teacher of not having "a clue" about what the
story in question.

154

I Had the Same Problem, Sir

When one of the "best students" reported that she was experiencing problems getting library materials for her assignment, another student, who from the view of others in the classroom had not even started his assignment, also claimed that it was difficult to get sources for his assignment. "I had the same problem, sir,." he claimed loudly.

There was a joking relationship between this student and others as they quietly questioned how much he had done and suggested that he had not even started his assignment.

Creative Bunch

In response to students' reasons for not having their homework completed on time, a teacher's remark that they were a "creative bunch" was, as evidenced by their immediate responses, considered humorous by the entire class. Even those who had jokingly been referred to as "creative" got comic relief from this evaluation.

In contrast to this situation, another teacher's warning to her class not to think of themselves as "too smart" to do the assigned work was not considered humorous.

Nothing

A teacher was asking specific questions to individual students to find out if they had studied an assigned poem.

At three different times during the class, the teacher directed a question to Mary. However, Mary did not respond to any of the teacher's questions.

When Mary did not respond to her third question the teacher demanded: "Mary, tell us what you learned about this poem." "Nothing," Mary quickly replied in a low voice.

Teacher and students laughed simultaneously at Mary's response. The teacher made light of Mary's response as she complimented her on her honesty.

Teacher and Student Identities

Although the examples of student humour pertaining to student and teacher identities show that to some extent such identities are negotiated in such episodes, the

155

suggestion here is that student identities seem to be more central in certain classroom episodes while the teacher's identity comes more to the fore in others. In other situations where teacher and/or student attempted to bring humour to bear on classroom life it would seem that the identities of both teachers and students are salient.

Any Intelligent Children

As a male teacher was writing the steps for solving a mathematics problem on the blackboard, he stood back for a moment and looked at what he was writing as if to determine what he had written was correct, or to ponder what the next step was. Much to the gratification of students, but to the chagrin of the teacher, one female student looked at the teacher and asked if his parents had any intelligent children.

Three days later this Level III student had a variation of her earlier question, this time for her female English teacher, as she inquired whether or not her parents had any good looking children.

While receiving a similar response from the students in English class as she did from those in the mathematics class, many of whom were the same students, the English teacher was seemingly less irritated by the question than the Mathematics teacher had appeared to be earlier.

Commentary
It was later learned that this student was perceived to be "a troublemaker" and as always attempting to taunt her teachers. Students and teachers alike reported that she was more successful in upsetting certain teachers than she was at disturbing others. While many students seemed to enjoy her humour in the two situations observed here, it is known that on other occasions some of the students did not see her actions as "funny". They empathized with the teacher who was the target of her humour.

What Am I Doing?

At different times during the early part of an English class, the teacher stopped her lesson and requested the class to pay more attention to what she was doing. At one point she told them to "be quiet" and later she demanded that they "stop talking".

156

Because some of the students did not obey her commands, she identified individuals in her attempt to curtail the noise level in the classroom.

Looking at one student she said: "John, sit in your seat and get your book out."

"Miss, what am I doing?" asked John, appearing surprised.

Some of those who were seated nearby laughed as John continued to declare his innocence of any wrong doing.

Reminding the Teacher

When a teacher forgot to collect assigned homework on the day it was due, many students thought this was a joke on the teacher. However, the attention quickly turned to the student who, after the class was over, reminded the teacher that he had forgotten to collect the homework that he had assigned for completion on that day.

CHAPTER 8

FORMS OF CLASSROOM HUMOUR

A review of the classroom humour recorded during the present observations in Atlantic Canada high schools suggests that humour is expressed in different, but not necessarily mutually exclusive, forms. This Chapter illustrates humour that is associated with the ambiguity of words, sarcasm, student wit, story telling, impersonation, practical jokes and nonverbal communications.

Ambiguity of Words

The ambiguity of words is a common source of classroom humour at the senior high school level. Examples of such humour observed in the present research include those associated with punning, homonyms, misunderstanding of what is said and playing on names.

Puns

One of the memorable examples of a pun was observed in a class where a music teacher was telling her students that they would have to study hard in preparation for the upcoming examinations. At the end of her suggestion for students to study, she said: "Music teachers give sound advice". Only a small number of students caught on to the pun without any prompting from others. "Getting in Tune" and "Short Story" are two other examples where punning was considered to be humorous.

Getting in Tune

Students, some of whom had just attended a music class, were gathering in the laboratory for a biology lesson. There was considerable talking among the students and many of them were acting, that is, had body movements, as if they were responding to music. The teacher told them to move more quickly to their seats and to get ready for the class. However, from his perspective, they did not respond positively to his request. At one point, he loudly proclaimed that if they did not "get in tune" they would "face the music".

Short Story

Background
Students in one Level I literature class knew that their teacher's favourite form of writing was the short story. Apparently, she often expressed this view to her students.

Episode
While returning a literature assignment to her class where students were to have written about the settings, characters and themes in selected readings, the teacher's major criticism seemed to be that many of the students did not elaborate enough on each of these elements. One student quickly interrupted the teacher's oral presentation on her evaluation of their assignments by noting that his reason for being brief was that he thought she liked "short stories". Spontaneous smiles, giggles, and laughter throughout the class were indicative of their appreciation of this student's observation.
The humour in this response was also appreciated by the teacher who smiled and then replied that the student was correct. However, she preceded to relate the difference between a short story and the need to give adequate responses to assignments such as the one she was returning to them.

Homonyms

Here is an example of humour that was created by two words with similar sounds.

Whether or Not

Background
As part of their education week activities, students from a Grade 10 classroom were preparing to dramatize a news/commentary programme following the format of a well known programme on

159

a local television channel. The dramatization was to include news, weather, sports and commentaries.

Episode
The class period observed was taken up with discussions about the dramatization of this programme. Some students volunteered for particular parts while others were asked to participate in specific roles. Earlier in the period Max agreed to report on the weather, another boy agreed to give the sports, and so. However, in the final minute or so of the 45 minute period, Max, who had earlier agreed to give the weather report, expressed some reservations about doing this report. Tony, looking at Max, asked: "You don't know whether or not you want to give the weather report?"
At least one student picked up this play on words. He laughed and repeated a version of the query "whether" or not Max would be doing the "weather" report in the drama. Other students and the teacher joined in the laughter, expressing their appreciation of the humour resulting in the use of these homonyms.

Misunderstandings

It is difficult to identify when there is misunderstanding between students and teachers in the classroom. Observations reveal that students sometimes pretend to misunderstand something the teacher has said, while in fact, they understand it perfectly well. This is one of the strategies they employ when they do not know the answer to a question. Teachers have also been observed to misunderstand what students said. One example of a teacher's misunderstanding that was perceived to be humorous is outlined in the "Outer Space" episode.

Outer Space

Background
There were 15 students in a literature class where the teacher was preparing the students to write short stories. Topics covered during this period included possible settings (time and place) for the stories, plot and character.

Episode
Students were suggesting possible setting such as in school, in a house, out of doors, in the city, or in a small community for their short stories.
One student informed the class that his story was to take place "down in the states."
The teacher pleasantly replied: "That's an idea, to have your story in outer space."
The fact that the teacher thought the student had said that his story was to take place "in outer space" provided comic relief as several of those present chuckled and inquired of the student what he had actually said.

Note
While it appears as if the students were entertained because the teacher did not correctly hear what the student had said, maybe there was something about the way student had spoken the words "down in the states" which had caused them to chuckle.

Playing on Names

While the process of playing on students' names with the intent of being funny

is not a widespread phenomena, it has been observed in different classrooms. One such

occurrence took place when a student, with the surname "Butt", was mocked by his peers for

his opposing their request for help with staging a play. The teacher observed that the student

was the "Butt of the joke". More often than not, the student who is the target of such jokes

reacts negatively to this type of play on their names.

Two Cents Worth

During a class discussion of the meanings found in a poem, a teacher looked at one student, who had not participated in the class discussion up to that point, and asked for her "two cents worth". The student did not have any verbal response for the teacher. However, she looked rather uncomfortable as two of her classmates were heard sniggering. Later, it was learned that the Christian name of the student who was asked for her two cents worth was "Penney" .

161

You Should Not Forget Her Name

Background
It was mid November when a student, whose family had just moved to the community, arrived at school. One of the teachers in the school was known for bicycle riding and also for seemingly forgetting students' names on different occasions.

Setting
As this teacher was introducing the new student to the class one of the students in the classroom jokingly suggested that teacher should not forget the name of the new student. Her name was Peddle.

Joyful

The teacher directed three female students to end their talk and laughter and get to work. However, from the teacher's point of view they did not comply with her request. She then looked at one of the girls and asked: "Why are you so joyful?" This girl's Christian name was Joy. She was not amused as the teacher, in her words, "tried to be funny."

To Make a Long Story Short

While not observed by the present researchers, one teacher told of a situation where the surnames "Short" and "Long" were found among students in the same classroom. She reported that both the students and teachers were known to have attempted to create humour with comments on these two names. Comments such as "to make a long story short" and "don't make your answers too long" were among those reported to have been used at one point or another in this class.

Two Kings

Setting
A Grade 12 class including two students with the surname "King".

Episode
Several of the students were, from the teacher's perspective, acting in a disorderly fashion during an English class. At different points during the early part of the class, the teacher

requested that they be quiet and more attentive. Among those students the teacher was experiencing difficulty bringing under control were the two King boys.
Much to the delight of a number of the students, a teacher observed that the class was lucky to have "two Kings in the one class".

Sarcasm

While the scornful and taunting tone of a sarcastic remark may be relatively easily identified, whether a remark expresses the opposite to what is literally said is often more difficult to ascertain. High school students not only complain about what they see as sarcastic and insulting remarks from teachers but tend to think that some teachers are predisposed to be sarcastic (see their comments in Chapter 6 of this book). Other teachers tend to be helpful and understanding (Martin, 1983). The present classrooms observations did not reveal anything to confirm or question this suggestion. However, teachers representing a number of schools in Atlantic Canada were observed being sarcastic. Whether or not the intent was to be funny was not always clear from those observations. It was obvious that those who received the brunt of sarcastic remarks were not unusually amused by them. On occasion, other student seemed to get a degree of satisfaction from such a situation.

A teacher's remark that he expected Barry to do better in the "I Expected Better Work from You" episode in the Student Identities section of Chapter 7 may well have been expressed with a tinge of sarcasm. The teacher's questions about female absenteeism as noted in the "Absenteeism" episode of Chapter 7 may also be seen as sarcasm. Another teacher was obviously sarcastic in his comment that a student's handwriting was beautiful when that student and everyone else in the class knew that the student's handwriting was very poor.

A situation that first brought laughter from students was quickly redefined by them when the teacher was viewed as having gone "too far" in his criticisms. He was thought to have been "insulting" and to be treating Sam "unfairly". Apparently, Sam was liked by most, if not all of the students in his class. He was perceived to be "different", but a "nice fellow". The students did not see him as a disruptive person or a troublemaker. The teacher could only go so far in "making fun" of Sam before other students empathized with him.

From Laughter to Insults

Setting
As the bell had rung, signalling that classes were to begin, students in a Level II history class were settling into their seats. Sam, one of the students, sat on his desk rather than on the accompanying chair. Even after the teacher had called the class to order and directed the class to the topic of the day's lesson, Sam remained on the desk for a moment or so before slowly getting off, seemingly intending to sit on the chair.

Student
Sam appeared to be older than most of his classmates. His hair was almost shoulder length, which was considerably longer than that of any other boys in the classroom. He was the only one in his class with a goatee. While his ear ring was not an unusual sight in this classroom, it was not a common practice among the boys in this school.

Episode
Before Sam sat on the chair, his teacher began to scold him for his slowness in becoming "properly" seated. Her reference to his slow movement and the fact that her scolding did not seem to have any influence on his behaviour brought laughter from a few of those present. However, the laughter soon disappeared as the teacher wondered how Sam was going to make out when

164

he was finished with school. At one point she asked: "What do
you think you are going to make of yourself?" The implication
was that he was "not going anywhere", not going to make
anything of himself, because "lazy people do not get very far."

The student who asked one of her teachers if his parents had any intelligent

children, as described in the "Any Intelligent Children" in the Teacher and Student Identities

section of Chapter 7, was obviously being sarcastic in her inquiry. Students have also been

observed making sarcastic remarks to each other. For example, one boy was sarcastic in his

suggestion that another boy in his class should be a cheerleader. This situation is outlined in

the "Joe Should Be A "Cheerleader" episode in the "Sex-Role Stereotyping" section of

Chapter 7.

Student Wit

A number of examples of student wit are found within the present chapter and

the preceding one. For example, "Napoleon's Age" in the curriculum section of Chapter 7,

and "Whether or Not," the example of a homonym given above, can be used to illustrate

student wit. Student wit covers a wide range of student responses. While certain student

responses, from their perspectives, may appear witty, they may be defined otherwise by

teachers, especially those with whom the student attempts to be witty. On occasion, student

wit is often in a good natured tone, while at other time it may be sarcastic and intended to

hurt. A teacher's appreciation of student wit, and what becomes defined by teachers and

students as witty, is influenced by a number of factors. Teacher appreciation of student wit

is seen in the "Apple Sauce" and "Where Do We Go from Here" situations described below.

These and other examples of wit have been observed providing comic relief from formal and

sometimes tension filled classroom settings.

165

Apple Sauce

Setting
Mathematics class where the teacher was correcting an assigned exercise on fractions. She was identifying individuals and requesting each to give his/her answer to specific problems.

Episode
The teacher asked Mary for her solution to the problem of dividing one full apple pie and one-half of another pie equally among six people. Much to the amusement of the whole class, except the teacher, Mary quickly replied: "Make apple sauce, Miss."

I Still Like It

The Grade 12 teacher could see he was losing his students. The students were obviously not attentive as the teacher delivered the day's Mathematics lesson. He decided to get the class more involved in the lesson, so he asked a boy in the front row: "Richard, have I influenced your attitude toward math?"
The boy thought about it for a moment, then smiled brightly and answered, "No sir, I still like it."
The whole class broke into laughter, including the teacher.

Note
This incident was not observed by the researcher, but told to him as a true story by the teacher in the class at the time.

Teed Off

Background
The biology teacher was well known for his interest in golf and as one who spent a considerable amount of time playing it.

Time
At the beginning of a biology lab.

Episode
After the teacher repeated the instructions to students for their biology laboratory, two students arrived late for the lab. The teacher was about mid way through the instructions for the third time when two more students came into the room. Apparently, the last two students to arrive had a reputation for being late for classes. The teacher interrupted his instructions to chastise them

166

for their tardiness. In response to the teacher's apparently
distraught behaviour over the fact that the students were coming
in late, despite earlier warnings about this behaviour, one boy in
the class was heard to comment: "Sir, you sound like you are
teed off."

Results
There was much laughter in the class. The teacher smiled, and
without continuing with the instructions for the lab, told the
class to get to work.

He Went on, and on, and,....

Background
From observations and interviews it was learned that several
students in one classroom experienced tension and were
apprehensive about giving a formal presentation to the class.
While most students followed the same relatively mechanistic
approach as they made their class presentations, one student,
who appeared to be more relaxed than others, inserted a little
humour into his talk to the class. This strategy was appreciated
by students and teacher alike.

Episode
An English teacher gave a "short story assignment" to one of
her classes. Each student was to select one story from a list
provided by the teacher, and to follow a set of guidelines for the
written assignment. Each student was also expected to share
his/her assignment through an oral presentation to the class. In
pointing to a weakness of the short story that he had studied,
one student reported that the author "went on, and on, and on,
and on,...." As the student slowly said these words, others in
the classroom -- including the teacher -- saw the humour in his
analysis and presentation.

Where Do We Go from Here?

There were about ten minutes left in the last period for the day
when the teacher had finished reviewing a unit in biology.
While checking some papers on his desk, the teacher asked, in
reference to the biology course: "Where do we go from here?"
The entire class was entertained when one student quickly
responded: "Home, sir."

The teacher laughed before he made brief comments on the next topics to be studied in biology.

The More You Talk the Better I Like It

Background
A class of Level II students had been given a number of topics from among which each student was to select one and do a "major" paper on it. Each student was expected to research the topic, do an oral presentation on it to the class, and submit a written paper to the teacher. Most of the students decided to do their papers on either resettlement or the cod moratorium.

Setting
It was the first class of three class periods where students were to make their oral presentations. The first student gave about a ten minute presentation which was interspersed with an occasional comment from the teacher. The teacher's comments were generally complimentary, but he did make some suggestions for improving content of the paper.

Episode
The second student had barely begun his presentation when the teacher made considerably more extensive comments than he had made regarding the first paper. At one point the teacher, apparently realizing that he was making unusually long comments, said: "I didn't mean to interrupt." He then instructed the student to "keep going" with his presentation. Much to the delight of others, this student replied: "The more you talk the better I like it."

Very Well Said

Setting
There were about 30 students in the classroom for a literature period. The first part of the class focused on the homework that had been assigned earlier. The teacher was identifying individual students and asking each to tell how he/she answered a homework question on a poem.

Episode
After the teacher had obtained responses from about six students, he asked John, who did not usually do too well on his homework, to read what he had written as the answer to the

168

homework question. John hesitated and replied that he had
nothing to add to what had already been noted by others.
Among his comments were: "It has already been very well
said." On this remark from John, several of the students in the
classroom laughed. They thought that John had not done as
well as some of those who had already given their responses to
the teacher, and he was attempting to give the impression that
he had covered most, if not all, of the points mentioned by other
students.

Story Telling

Like other forms of classroom humour, there is a wide range of strategies in

story telling. A teacher may, for example, tell a humorous story in reference to him/herself.

Such was the case in the "time keeper" story below. They may tell a story in reference to a

student. See, for example, the "I still like it" episode presented in the student wit section

above.

Time Keeper

At the beginning of the class, on the day after the school
volleyball team had lost several of the games in the regional
tournament, the teacher told of his experience in sports at
university. He reported that he wanted to be a runner and
participate in other track and field events. However, one day
his coach had called him aside and told him that he would make
more of contribution to the team if he would become a time
keeper.

The example of "a television joke", given earlier (Chapter 7), illustrates that

teachers sometimes tell stories without any reference to the formal curriculum being taught at

the time. In fact, the joke which the teacher reported hearing on television seemingly had no

bearing the mathematics which he was reviewing with the class. From this and other

incidents, the implication is that, if it is to be effective, story telling should be related to the

169

formal or informal curriculum taught at the time or be blended into the interaction dynamics of the classroom at the time of its occurrence.

Then He Created Woman

Setting
A Religious education class where the issue of creation was raised, although it was not part of the original lesson plan. The teacher told the following story to his class.

Story
After God created man, he took a look at him and said: "I know I can do a better job than this." He then created woman.

Results
It seemed as if the entire class laughed at this story. After the laughter subsided, the girls continued, even after the period had ended, to remind the boys of the reason why women are "better than", "superior to", and "smarter than" men.

Impersonations

Another strategy commonly used by students in their attempts to inject humour into the classroom is that of impersonation. While impersonating mass media stars has been observed in a number of school settings, and it often wins students the attention of their peers, the present research suggests that teachers and school administrators are the most frequent targets of student impersonations. Even though such impersonations are more often than not spontaneous and brief, they bring considerable comic relief among students. Teacher characteristics that students have been observed impersonating include style of walking, body movement while teaching (e.g., head movement), hand in pocket, facial expression (e.g., stern looks and artificial smile, and manner of speech (e.g., "Now class let's get down to business;" "You know what I mean;" "Be quiet").

170

As revealed by their comments that students "make fun" of them and "imitate their mannerism" to provide fun for others, teachers are well aware of the fact that students impersonate them. However, given the subtle nature and brevity of most of the students' performances, teachers, and many of the students, are not always cognizant of the specific situations where impersonations occur. An example may be provided, however, of a situation where all the students present as well as their teacher quickly realized that a student was impersonating the teacher who was in the classroom at the time. Both students and teacher appeared to get considerable enjoyment out of this student act. One Grade 12 boy often created humour by pretending to walk like one of the male teachers, while simultaneously having one hand in his pocket jingling money in a manner similar to the teacher's. This imitation was done in ridicule. This boy was also known for his imitations of other teachers.

Among the impersonations observed in the present research were students imitating particular characteristics of television personalities. For example, one boy's imitation of Mr. Roper, a familiar television character in the early and mid 1980s, was a source of laughter on different occasions. A high school girl's imitation of Roseanne Arnold was considered funny by a small group of girls prior to the beginning of a class.

Practical Joke

It would seem that practical jokes have been a part of classroom life from the beginning. Oral tradition includes many stories about placing thumb tacks on the teacher's or a fellow student's seat. Sneaking an insect under the bell on the teacher's desk and situating a spider in the among the books of a female student were practical jokes of

171

yesterdays classrooms. The present study did not uncover many instances of practical jokes in the high schools of Atlantic Canada. In fact, only three examples of this form of humour were recorded. On one occasion, a male student hid a female student's books. This may have been a joke to others, but it had no humour for the victims of the practical joke. On another occasion, a Grade 12 male removed the books from one student's desk and placed them in that of another. When the students whose books had been exchanged learned of the mischief, they immediately took action against the suspect because "he is always doing something crazy". Another student incorporated a unique practical joke in a geology assignment -- a concrete sample.

A Concrete Sample

Among the sample of rocks which one student jokingly brought
to school as part of an assignment in geology was a piece of
concrete.
"What kind of a rock is this?" the teacher asked. The student
had no reply.
The teacher smilingly said that it was "a concrete sample".
Much to the delight of others, including the teacher, another
student quickly asked: "A concrete sample of what?"

Nonverbal Humour

At the outset it should be noted that each of the verbal forms of humour illustrated to this point undoubtedly included some aspect of nonverbal behaviour as it developed and unfolded. Aside from these nonverbal communications, there is a wide range of nonverbal classroom humour. Given the impossibility of observing everything that may be going on in a classroom at a given time, it is likely that some of this humour would go unnoticed, even to the most astute observer sitting in a classroom of 20 or more high school students. However, the present classroom observations alerted us to some of the nonverbal

172

behaviours that students, judging from their smiles, giggles, snickers and laughter, students found to be funny at one time or another. One student's inattentiveness, as suggested by his slumping to his seat, was greeted with smiles from a small number of his peers. Another student got the attention of others, some of whom laughed at him, when he made more than the normal amount of noise in moving his books from his desk and placing them on the floor by his seat. A third student, who fell asleep during class time, was awakened by the laughter that erupted when others realized that he was sleeping.

Another example of nonverbal humour was observed in a Level II classroom where many of the students tittered as one of the boys left his seat and pushed a girl who was sitting in an adjacent row. The boy had returned to his seat and was pretending to be innocent when the teacher, realizing someone was misbehaving, stopped writing on the blackboard and sternly looked at the class.

While no such incident of humour was recorded during the present classroom observations, it is speculated that quite apart from being an element in impersonation body language, such as grimaces, arm movements and walking may, raise a laugh in the classroom.

PART 1V

PRACTICE AND THEORY OF CLASSROOM HUMOUR

By drawing on the review of the literature presented earlier in this book (Chapter 1), and by selecting aspects of the findings on student views on school humour in Atlantic Canada (Chapters 3 through 6), the first chapter in this part of the book identifies the potentially positive (constructive) and potentially negative (destructive) features of classroom humour. The final task of this book, undertaken in the final chapter, is to move to another level of analysis and to offer suggestions relating to the concepts and issues that need to be considered in developing a sociological theory of classroom humour.

CHAPTER 9

FUNCTIONS OF CLASSROOM HUMOUR

The pitfalls of focusing on the functions of classroom humour include those which have been enunciated over the years as weaknesses of a structural functionalist approach in the study of social organizations. One problem of this focus is its susceptibility to teleological explanations, that is, its reasoning that developments within a social system have their origins in the purpose they serve. With reference to classroom humour, the argument would be that classroom humour by its very presence, by the fact that it developed in this setting, serves a function. Conversely, the argument is that if humour is not present within a classroom it is because it has no function within this setting. The present writers do not adhere to this line of thought and, without becoming preoccupied with this doctrine of final causes, the intent of the present chapter is to summarize the positive social functions of classroom humour as alluded to throughout this book and to note the potentially destructive side of this dimension of classroom culture. A concluding note is given on the desirability of keeping a balance between the humorous and the sterner approaches in the classroom.

Positive Humour

By way of highlighting the positive functions of classroom humour, reference is made here to earlier writings. Then, our attention turns to the positive functions of classroom humour as seen from the perspectives of high school students in Atlantic Canada.

Earlier Research

The literature relating to the functions humour is revealing in that people in different disciplines have given considerable effort to isolating what they see as the many positive functions of this dimension of human life. Some of the far reaching claims concerning the functions of humour include its reflection of the human side of people, its liberating effects, its alleviating of fears and anxiety, and its enhancing of interpersonal relations. Humour has been seen as a resource for integrating, differentiating, or constraining social relationships and as a means of developing and protecting one's self-concept.

Martineau (1972) identified three broad functions of humour as conflict humour, control humour and consensual humour. Social comic relief is another function of humour. Comic relief gives respite from the seriousness of the immediate situation. In so doing it may brighten the attitudes of the participants and thereby contribute to the successful completion of the task at hand.

Nilsen's (1993:287-296) review of humour theory points to the physiological functions of exhilaration, relaxation and healing; to the psychological functions of relief, ego defense, coping and gaining status; to the educational functions of alertness, arguing and persuading, teaching effectively and long-term-memory learning; and to the social functions of in-bonding, out-bonding, promoting social stability, and promoting social change. Within a sociological orientation to humour, Koller (1988:17-29) discussed a wide range of social functions of humour including that of social bonding, providing relief from stress and strain, expressing aggression or hostility, a forum for librating life, a process of self-effacement, a means of social correction and upholding honesty over sham, a mechanism for provoking

178

thought, an opportunity for balancing pain, the potential of reinforcing or undermining stereotypes, a method of therapy or catharsis, a way of defending against, countering or parrying attacks or threats, and a strategy of survival. The positive functions of humour in general have been said to include creating a feeling of goodwill among the participants in the setting, facilitating communications, promoting flexibility in relationships, bringing otherwise unexpressed attitudes and feelings into focus, breaking impasses, and creating a relaxed atmosphere.

Classroom humour has an important role in nurturing an open, warm and friendly climate in this setting. Some researchers have found that humour is positively associated with student creativity and the retention of subject matter taught in the school. Humour has been seen as both a coping and a distancing mechanism for students. It is a coping mechanism in that it can be a forum for students to share personal problems. In addition, it is a coping mechanism as students express their resistance to the school structure. Under such circumstances, the humour may be hostile and create problems for teachers and other students in the classroom. Students have also been known to joke about a crisis in order to distance themselves from the crisis.

Teacher initiated humour can serve a number of positive functions. For example, it has been known to facilitate harmonious relationships. Humour is also a way for teachers to gain status in the classroom. Self-disparaging jokes have been shown to enhance a teacher's sense of control in the classroom, while simultaneously helping students to remember what is being taught. On the other hand, such jokes may undermine the control which teachers may have, especially in classrooms where the objectives of schooling are not in line with those of the out-of-school culture of the students.

The Student Perspective

There is a commonly held view among high school students in Atlantic Canada that teaching-learning processes benefit from a "fun atmosphere" in the school in general and in the classroom in particular. Fellow students and teachers alike are believed to have important roles in reducing the social distances between teachers and students, thereby creating a positive school spirit. Such a school spirit is necessary for reciprocal joking relationships. A good sense of humour has been identified by high school schools to be a highly desirable teacher characteristic. Suggestions among students relating to the presence of a sense of humour include that it is associated with (1) age of teacher (younger teachers tend to be more humorous than the older ones); (2) teacher perception of student maturity (greater maturity is more conducive to teacher fostering humour in teacher-student interaction); and (3) teacher gender (though no consensus was discovered on whether male or female teachers initiate more humour).

Students identified a number of benefits from having humour as an integral part of school culture. The presence of humour as an accepted part of teacher-student interactions could (1) show the human side of teachers, (2) "bring" teachers "down" to the level of the students, (3) enhance student-teacher relationships, (4) generate positive attitudes toward teachers, (5) break the monotony of classroom life, (6) contribute to student enjoyment of what is being taught, (7) induce students into liking the subject taught at the time, (8) stimulate or maintain student interest in the lesson, (9) make learning more fun, and (10) make learning easier.

No Laughing Matter

Similar to our discussion of the positive functions of classroom humour, this review of the negative consequences of humour first deals with earlier writings and then highlights the concerns of high school students in Atlantic Canada relating to the negative features of classroom humour.

Earlier Research

It is no laughing matter when humour, initiated by either the teacher or the student at the beginning of the class, sets the wrong tone for the class; under such circumstances, the teacher has little control and teaching-learning process is stifled. Similarly, continuous joking, for example, story telling and practical jokes, is not advantageous to the teaching-learning process. Different writers have also noted that sarcasm, making fun of students, and using taboo language are no laughing matters in terms of maximizing the overall benefits of teaching and learning in the classroom. While hostile student humour, that is, humour that reflects a resistance to the school structure, may give pleasure to some students, it is often no laughing matter with respect to the aims of schooling and the development of desirable school-community relationships.

The Student Perspective

Given the theoretical orientation of the present research into the schooling experiences of high school students, it is not surprising to see that students often have views which are in sharp contrast to those of their teachers. On occasion, this contrast is vividly

181

seen in meanings which teachers and students have for humour; what is humorous for one may be no laughing matter for the other. From the student perspective, there is no fun in the classroom where joking relationships between teachers and students are not reciprocal; teachers must be willing to take a joke as well as give one.

In the opinion of some students, the negative consequences of classroom humour include the tendency for some teachers to waste time as they "stray" from the subject with their injection of humour into the lesson, and the waste of both teaching time and students' time for learning with the excessive "joking round" by teachers. Students have also reported that, on occasion, they are hesitant to take a more active role in classroom situations because they are afraid that the teacher would "make fun of them". It is not surprising to learn that when teachers persistently tell what students perceive to be "boring" or "stupid" jokes students tend to lose interested in classroom activities.

Students are generally very unhappy with teachers who are seen to treat students differently with respect to joking relationships in the classroom. Frequent joking with some while continuously ignoring others is not usually given a positive review. Reinforcing humour-related actions of only few students while ignoring, discouraging and, even punishing, similar actions of others is no laughing matter for those who see themselves as victims of teachers' discriminatory actions.

Sarcastic and insulting teachers do not provide comic relief by their hurtful remarks. Students in the present study specifically noted their displeasure with teachers who sought to be funny as they put down students in the presence of others in connection with incorrect answers, student dress and private matters. Many students expressed the view that

182

such demeaning actions are often associated with teachers' moods. Conversely, students have noted that the mood of the student is often an important factor in the meanings which they give to teachers and teachers' actions. While students have been known to make fun of teachers who are humourless, generally speaking it is no laughing matter when teachers do not have a sense of humour.

KEEPING A BALANCE

One overriding theme in students' perspectives on school humour in Atlantic Canada may be encapsulated as a desire for teachers to keep a balance between humorous and stern strategies in their dealings with students. Students report comparing humorous teachers to the serious ones. Having a good of sense of humour is a desirable characteristic of a high school teacher. Conversely, teachers who do not have a sense of humour do not receive such positive evaluation from their students. Those who lack a sense of humour are often viewed as being either too serious, too boring, too stern or too strict. From the student perspective, as a general rule, teachers should employ a balance of humour and more solemn strategies in the classroom. But, as noted at different points in the present review of students' views of school humour (Chapters 3-6) and during the analysis of the context and form of classroom humour (Chapters 7-8), whether or not humour is successful in a given situation depends on a combination of factors including the meanings which teachers and students give to the situation. These meanings are influenced by, and they influence, the teacher and student identities which are salient at the time. While describing classroom interaction as fitting somewhere on a continuum ranging from humorous to serious may be helpful in understanding the general nature of the social climate in this setting, a caveat is needed to this approach. In order to maximize the benefits of humour for teaching-learning processes, humour must be taken seriously. Teachers would be well advised to remember that it is important to "jest" for the fun of it, and to "jest" to be serious.

Taking Humour Seriously

To elaborate on the idea of taking humour seriously, the present study highlights the importance of a sense of humour in different dimensions of schooling including the development and maintenance of a positive school climate, the fostering of student creativity, and the enhancement of student learning. As indicated from their responses to a request for them to comment on anything about their schooling experiences which concern them, many high school students in Atlantic Canada would argue that teachers who employ humour in the classroom are often more serious about the teaching-learning endeavour than they would at first appear to be. In fact, some students are of the opinion that teachers who employ humour in their interactions with students are more serious, more concerned, about student welfare and learning than teachers who approach teaching in an authoritarian and stern manner.

As well as acknowledging the need to encourage teachers informally to develop a sense of humour in their teaching, some educators have advocated the inclusion of instructional materials on how to use humour in the formal education of teachers, administrators and school counsellors.

In addition to, yet not totally separate from, the practical implications of understanding classroom humour in terms of the positive and negative functions of humour in

184

this setting, there is the issue of developing a sociological theory of classroom humour. This problem is addressed in our final chapter.

CHAPTER 10

TOWARD A SOCIOLOGICAL THEORY
OF CLASSROOM HUMOUR

There is a range of views on the desirability and feasibility of developing a
theory of humour. For example, with respect to humour in psychotherapy, one writer
observed that it is not restricted to any theoretical framework (Salameh, 1983:62). Those
who are humorously endowed use it naturally without seeking theoretical or other
justifications. Others have offered theoretical notes, mainly within psychology, relating to
the presence and purpose of intergroup humour (e.g., Goldstein, 1976). Even though there
have been considerable developments with respect to theories of, and research on, humour
since Dodge and Rossett (1982:11) complained of a lack of good theory development, the
sociological intricacies of humour, particularly in educational settings, have not been fully
identified. Given the fact that humour by its very nature involves social interactions,
meanings and social identities, concepts which are central to sociology, it is suggested here
that sociology has much to contribute to our understanding of this phenomenon. With
reference to developing a sociological theory of classroom humour, we propose that an
inductive approach to theory building would be a meaningful route to pursue. By way of
adding to our understanding of the complexities of humour as a means of communicating, to
our desire to identify the potential of humour for the overall nature of social interactions, and
to our appreciation of how humour may facilitate the goals of teaching-learning situations,
this chapter focuses on three major topics, each with its own categories, as one moves
toward developing a substantive theory of classroom humour: (1) experiencing classroom

humour -- subjective reality, social context and forms of humour; (2) categories of classroom humour -- resistance humour, crisis humour and integrating humour; and (3) humour as process and product -- student self-development, teacher identity and hidden curriculum. The final task of this chapter is to offer some concluding remarks on the promise of an inductive-interpretative approach to understanding classroom humour.

An Inductive Approach

Induction is the logical process of developing generalizations from specific examples, of going from single instances to general principles. It is the process of building a theory from empirical observations or measurements. A distinction has been made between enumerative induction, that is generalizations based on statistical probability, and analytic induction, where individual cases are examined to identify their essential characteristics and on that basis to develop theoretical categories and propositions. The idea is to develop theory that is grounded in data, rather than starting with a theory and then attempting to verify it. The study of classroom humour, as is the case in the present research, could lead to the development of a substantive theory relating to this phenomenon. In this respect, the idea of a formal theory is reserved for a conceptual area, such as socialization and power, of sociological inquiry. The study of humour itself might qualify as such a conceptual area of inquiry, but by limiting the research to classroom humour, specifically to high school classrooms, any theoretical development that takes place is within the substantive domain.

The combination of an analytic inductive method and a focus on the subjective realities of the actors in a particular setting leads one to an intensive study of the ways those actors experience that setting, to their social construction of reality. In reference to the study

187

of classroom humour, the challenge is to identify how students and teachers experience this dimension of classroom culture, that is, their meanings of humour; to identify categories of classroom humour, and to understand humour as a process in, and a product of, teacher-student interactions. These dimensions of classroom humour are suggestive of the sources and the results of laughter in this setting.

Experiencing Classroom Humour

In line with Fine's (1977:315) observation that humour is a delicate flower, a living bud which when plucked quickly dies, an underlying assumption of the present focus on classroom humour is that it be studied in its natural environment. Three intertwined dimensions of this stance need to considered: the subjective realities of the participants in the setting, the social context of the humour and the form in which it gets played out.

Subjective Reality

An underlying assumption of the subjective reality approach which guides the present study of school humour is that reality is socially constructed by the participants in the day-to-day interactions in the school. While there have been certain general guidelines as to what constitutes humour in the classroom, and while there are commonly accepted parameters within which humour develops in this setting, there is no universally accepted definition of what words, acts, events or sequence of events will be seen as humorous in the classroom. The assumption is that there is nothing inherent in a happening that makes it humorous. It should be noted, however, that this is not to suggest that certain types of classroom humour do not become institutionalized. There is a connection between the subjective realities of the classroom and the objective realities of the larger societal and

188

cultural environments in which the school is placed. These environments may be seen to be mediated through the social organization of schooling that help shape and reshape the daily lives of students and teachers. However, it is clear that what is perceived to be humorous by one group of students may not be defined as such by other students, even within the same classroom at the time. And, as expected, what is humorous for some students is not always viewed as such by their teachers. This situation is accommodated within the stance of the interpretative tradition in sociology of not imposing some objective meaning of classroom humour when studying this phenomenon. In other words, the subjective reality approach focuses on the meanings and interpretations which students and teachers have for one another and for happenings in the classroom at a particular time. Intertwined with these interpretations and meanings are the identities which each actor has of himself or herself. Simultaneously, the social context must be considered to the extent that it interfaces with the development and expression of humour in this setting.

Social Context

Even though the subjective reality of classroom humour is, by definition, humour as experienced by the participants in this setting, and though there may be multiple realities at one time in this setting, the social context of the classroom is of considerable relevance to the nature and extent of classroom humour. Institutional characteristics relating to the family, mass media, sports, sex-role stereotyping and politics are among the major dimensions of the social context evidenced in different episodes of classroom humour observed in the present research. The legal-rational authority of teachers and their expertise in matters evolving round the formal curriculum were seen to be part of the organizational domain which had a bearing on the development of classroom humour. Another organizational feature that is significant in classroom humour is the demarcation between class time and other time. The different moods associated with beginning, middle and ending of class periods also seem to influence the interaction processes associated with humour. The environment within the school itself may also be revealed in the playing out of humour in the classroom. The present research found as well that classroom humour may develop in reference to the formal curriculum. More specifically, episodes of humour have been seen to develop around topics in History, Literature, Science, Mathematics and Religion.

A more complete understanding of the social context of classroom humour would necessitate a study of other variables that may be associated with humour in this setting. For example, humour appears to be associated with age in that each age-group develops humour that reflect the social characteristics ascribed to it. The humour of adolescence takes on different forms, and serves different functions, from that of childhood or adulthood. Gender may be another variable influencing classroom humour.

Forms of Humour

Classroom observations reveal that there are several dominant forms of humour in teacher-student interactions. One group of forms relates to the ambiguity of words, puns and homonyms have been known to create humour for both students and teachers in the classroom. The classroom is also fertile ground for misunderstandings in teacher-student communications, misunderstandings which produce humour at least for some participants in the interactions. Also, in relation to the meanings of words, teachers have been observed commenting on students' names in a jocular way. Although such comments are sometimes perceived to be funny by the student, more often than not they cause displeasure among the students. Similarly, teacher sarcasm can be a sort of humour for teachers, but it is not usually seen as funny by students. While storytelling as a form of humour has been observed in high schools in Atlantic Canada, it is not a common form of classroom humour.

Student wit, their impersonating of others and playing practical jokes on each other and their teachers have been observed creating humour for students and teachers in the classroom.

Categories of Classroom Humour

At another level of analysis, the present data indicates that classroom humour can be categorized according to context of self-processes within the classroom. Both students and teacher develop particular identities in relation to each other, and there are continuous processes at work as they carve out their respective interactive roles and agendas. Focusing on students, it is seen that they initiate humour as a resistance to the organizational constraints of teachers' authority and expertise. Student humour may also be a response to crises they are experiencing in the school. However, not all humour is either resistance humour or crisis humour. Some humour is a part of the ebb and flow of the day-to-day interactions within the classroom. It is described here as integrating humour. The boundaries of separating one of these categories of humour from the other two are not always clear in the subjective realities of classroom life, but they are addressed separately here for analytic and presentational clarity.

Resistance Humour

As defined by McLaren (1986) and Woods (1990) resistance humour occurs when an entire class or a significant number of students turn against the teacher. The intent is to mock or to denounce the teacher. No example of this ideal type of resistance humour was observed in the present research. However, when humour that disrupts the flow of teaching and learning is seen as resistance humour, one can easily find examples in the school. To illustrate, the students who continued to laugh, joke and clown round rather than obey their biology teachers' instructions to get ready for the formal class may be seen as employing resistance humour at the time. One student in particular was less attentive than others, that is, he was more resistant to the teacher's authority. His resistance elicited a suggestion from the teacher that he was just like his brother and hence the humour in the situation ("You Are Just Like Your Brother" episode Chapter 7). Similarly, one student's slowness in becoming properly seated at the beginning of a class as described in the episode "From Laughter to Insults" (Chapter 8) may be seen as his resistance to the teacher expectations for students to be promptly seated when the bell indicates classes are to begin.

Students in different schools have been observed attempting to get others to laugh at their behaviours and at teachers' reactions to them. While such actions may be interpreted as a strategy for getting acceptance from one's peers, it is simultaneously a way of resisting the formal organizational and curriculum domains within school culture.

Classroom observations reveal that one or another form of humour is a common practice among misbehaving students. These practices are known to include students' talking in a jovial manner, playing jokes on each other, grimacing, and making fun of the appearances and actions of others.

Crisis Humour

As identified in the present research, crisis humour arises as a way of dealing with a perceived threat to one's identity in the situation. Both students and teachers engage in this form of humour.

While some students may, on occasion, enjoy the situation where a teacher attempts to highlight his/her failure to do the assigned work or his/her poor performance on an examination, such public ridicule is not widely considered as funny. On the contrary, the resulting student embarrassment and the meanings which they attributed to teacher's action may have devastating effects on student-teacher interactions including the students becoming engaged in crisis humour. When a teacher's reference to specific students is not intended to be humorous, other students may take advantage of the situation to make fun of, to laugh at, the behaviour of their peers in the classroom. From the student perspective, then, crisis humour may be seen as a means of providing relief from teacher sarcasm and ridicule, from unequal treatment received at the hands of the teacher and from peer pressure. In other words, it is a way of coping with the frustrations that may be associated with not performing, academically and socially, at the level expected of the student.

For teachers, crisis humour may help release tension inducted by work expectations and the subsequent fatigue experienced in the classroom. Such a role occurs, for instance, when the teacher tells "funny" stories. One such example may be the "Television Joke" (Chapter 7). This joke had no apparent connection with the lesson taught

193

at the time. Stories that are tied in with the happenings in the classroom, for example, the "Time Keeper" and "Then He Created Woman" episodes in Chapter 8, may also be a reflection of mechanisms whereby teachers cope with stresses of classroom life.

For both students and teachers, the joke, the fun and the laughter in crisis humour frequently camouflage the seriousness of the situation. It is a way of distancing oneself from the hurt one is feeling and from a threat to one's self-concept, thereby enabling classroom interactions to continue with the least amount disruptions and overt displeasure.

Integrating Humour

Although resistance humour and crisis humour are core elements in classroom culture, a considerable portion of classroom laughter is not necessarily evidence of a resistance to the teacher, to the school organization or to the formal curriculum. Neither is it indicative of crises in the classroom lives of students or teachers. Instead, much classroom laughter may be referred to as communal laughter in that students are brought together in a happy atmosphere. Since it brings people together this type of humour is referred to here as integrating humour. In fact, crisis humour may also serve an integrating function. To highlight the distinction between the two it is noted that crisis humour arises, as the name suggests, from a crisis, be it large or small, in one's classroom life. There is a perceived threat to one's identity and/or to one's plan of action. Integrating humour, on the other hand, arises without such a crisis. It can occur spontaneously in warm, close and more or less informal classroom interactions. One example of integrated humour from the present research is the laughter that followed the practical joke of one student who, when asked to bring different samples of rocks to his geology class, brought a piece of concrete to his class

194

as "a concrete example". Students' responses to a teacher's comments that the classroom needs a revolving door to accommodate the students who were frequently coming and going during school hours is another example of integrating humour. Similarly, when a teacher joined his students in making disparaging comments about the cafeteria food the resulting laughter had an integrating effect on teacher-student relationships.

Integrating humour provides an opportunity for students, who are otherwise in competition with each other, to come together and share experiences in the classroom. It can bring fun and lightness into a class that may be generally be filled with seriousness and tension. Such humour also offers an outlet for students' wit and another means of getting recognition in this setting.

Humour as Process and Product

Classroom humour can be viewed as a part of the process of the developing social order within the classroom, a process of self-development for students, a process of identity formation and identity maintenance for teachers, and a process of teaching and learning dimensions of life that are not set out in the formal curriculum. Simultaneously, humour is a product of student self-development, of teacher identities and of things previously learned from the hidden curriculum.

Student Self-Development

An overriding theme in student self-development with respect to classroom humour may be encompassed in the concept of impression management. To elaborate, impression management refers to the processes whereby one manages the situation so that one will be seen in a favourable light by significant others. Even casual observations reveal that this is a

195

common process among high school students in the teaching-learning environment of the classroom. Several strategies may be employed within the general rubric of impression management. One of those is that of student pretence. On different occasions, students have been observed pretending to be innocent of the misbehaviour of which they have been accused. While such pretence does not always result in humour, laughter is often created in the classroom by students who pretend to be innocent of "acting up", or "misbehaving", or "interrupting" the teaching-learning process. One illustration of such student pretence is seen in the "Why Do You Ask Me?" episode, where a student pretended to be innocent when a teacher implied that he was misbehaving. Another, but different, illustration is the "Something in My Throat" episode, where a student pretended to have something in his throat. Perhaps this student was seeking attention or attempting to avoid answering a teacher's question. A third example of pretence is described in the "A Studious Front" episode where a student pretended to be giving information on something which the teacher accused him of not having a clue about (Details of these illustration of pretence are given in Chapter 7).

Sometimes humour is created because teachers are perceived to be pretending. Such an example is described in "A Mistake" in Chapter 7. In that situation students perceived that one of their teachers had made a mistake in explaining an algebraic problem, while the teacher claimed to have intentionally put incorrect information on the blackboard. The mistake episode is also an illustration of the importance teachers attach to presenting to the class what they see as an appropriate identity.

Teacher Identity

While not the focus of the present research, the importance of teacher identity was evident in much of classroom humour observed in high schools of Atlantic Canada. At the outset it must be noted that individual teachers often make reference to themselves during the playing out of humour. More specifically, two groupings of teacher self-references have been known to add a dimension of humour to the classroom. One of these groupings includes teachers' deprecating comments on themselves. The other references are the self-extolling descriptions. It is noted that while teacher self-deprecation is more often than not an integral part of classroom humour, self-extolling situations are often not seen in this way.

A teacher's story, from his university days, of how his coach, suggested that he would make more of a contribution as a "Time Keeper" (Chapter 8) to the track and field team than as a member of that team was told in a self-deprecatory manner, and it had the desired effect of generating empathy with the students whose volleyball team had lost several games in a regional tournament.

From the student perspective, certain teachers are sometimes seen as extolling themselves. Such actions, although they may be conceived in jest, are not usually perceived as such by students. More often than not they are sources of annoyance to students who, in turn, find ingenious ways of responding to them. Perhaps, the episodes "A Mistake", "Troublesome Words" and "Any Intelligent Children" in Chapter 7 are examples of students' responses to teachers' self-righteous demeanour and aloofness in the school.

Hidden Curriculum

The fact that students learn many things in school which are not part of the formal curriculum has been the focus of considerable attention in the sociology of education. Indeed, a number of dimensions of this aspect of schooling have been brought to the front by different sociological perspectives (Baksh, 1990). Symbolic interactionism highlights the multiplicity of meanings which students have regarding the organizational, curriculum and action domains of schooling. Focusing on classroom humour, it is likely that most, if not all, humorous situations have many meanings for students, many hidden messages, that is, messages which were not intended by the originator of the humour. The present research identified some of the meanings which students gave to classroom humour observed, in addition to identifying the fact that they perceived such episodes as humorous. It is not difficult to imagine the types of messages which students may attach to specific situations. The most obvious messages, perhaps not hidden at all, are those associated with the sex-role stereotyping humour as illustrated in the examples of "Absenteeism", "Hockey Equipment", "Joe Should be a Cheerleader" and "The Bottom Line" of Chapter 7. One teacher's view on the desirable number of political parties in a democracy may be gleaned from his observation that there were too many parties in the Canadian federal election that was in progress when this observation was made (see "Too Many Parties" in Chapter 7). Other messages hidden within different episodes of classroom humour relate to the rules, routines and regulations of classroom life, to the beliefs and opinions of teachers, and to the values embodied in the formal curriculum.

Concluding Remarks

By way of concluding this study of school humour and the present chapter on moving toward a sociological theory of classroom humour, a few remarks on the promise of the inductive-interpretative approach in the study of classroom humour are in order   In applying the strengths of symbolic interactionism as identified by Hargreaves (1978) to the study of school humour we suggest that this approach has (1) an appreciative capacity -- the capacity to explore humour from the point of view of students, teachers and school personnel; (2) a designatory capacity -- the capacity to articulate taken-for-granted commonsense knowledge about the place of humour in interpersonal relationships in the school and in teaching-learning processes; (3) a reflective capacity -- the ability to provide students, teachers and others with the means to reflect on their own activities; (4) an immunological capacity -- the potential to inform school and classroom policy with knowledge and understanding of the everyday life of those within these settings; and (5) a corrective capacity -- the ability to critique theories that are not grounded in the bedrock reality of school and classroom life. Woods (1990:392-393) added four other, but interrelated, strengths of the inductive-interpretative approach as represented in symbolic interactionism: (6) its illuminative capacity -- the potential to provide a broad range, considerable depth and a richness of detail on all aspects of humour in the school; (7) its theoretical capacity -- the process of generating theory inductively which leads to the development of strongly grounded theory and possibility of interfacing between the process of classroom humour (micro theory) and the institutional and organizational contexts (macro theory) of this humour; (8) its policy-making capacity -- the capacity to impact on policies relating to sex-role stereotyping or to other messages in the hidden, and not so hidden, curriculum and to teacher education as it deals with interpersonal relationships in the school and with teaching-learning strategies; and (9) its collaborative capacity -- the opportunity for teachers, administrators and school counsellors to collaborate with researchers in studying the micro level processes of interactions in the school, thereby raising the potential of effecting change from within the classroom.

REFERENCES

Adams, Richard C.
    1972   "Is Physics a Laughing Matter?" *The Physics Teacher*, Vol 10. No 5 (May). Pp. 265-266.

Armour, Richard
    1975   "Humour in the Classroom." *The Independent School Bulletin*. October, p. 61.

Baksh, Ishmael J.
    1990   "The Hidden Curriculum." Pp. 170-189 in Orteza y Miranda and Magsino, Romulo F. (Eds.) *Teaching, Schools and Society*. London: The Falmer Press.

Baksh, Ishmael J. and Martin, Wilfred B.W.
    1983   *Teacher Expectation and the Student Perspective*. St. John's: Publications Committee, Faculty of Education, Memorial University of Newfoundland.

    1986   *Teaching Strategies: The Student Perspective*. St. John's: Publications Committee, Faculty of Education, Memorial University of Newfoundland.

    1992   *Gender Differences in Students' Perceptions of Schooling*. St. John's: Publications Committee, Faculty of Education, Memorial University of Newfoundland.

Beynon, John
    1985   *Initial Encounters in the Secondary School*. London: The Falmer Press.

Beynon, John and Atkinson, Paul
    1984   "Pupils as Data-Gatherers: Mucking and Sussing." Pp. 255-272 in Sara Delamont (ed.) *Readings on Interaction in the Classroom*. London: Methuen.

Blumer, Herbert
    1969   *Symbolic Interactionism: Perspective and Method*. Englewood Cliffs, New Jersey: Prentice-Hall, Inc.

Bryant, Jennings, Comisky, Paul W., Crane, Jon S. and Zillmann, Dolf
    1980   "Relationship Between College Teachers' Use of Humor in the Classroom and Students' Evaluations of Their Teachers." *Journal of Educational Psychology*, Vol. 72, No. 4, pp. 511-519.

202

Crabbs, Michael A., Crabbs, Susan K. and Goodman, Joel
    1986   "Giving the Gift of Humor (Ho, Ho, Ho): An Interview with Joel
            Goodman." *Elementary School Guidance & Counselling*. December, pp.
            105-113.

Chapman, Antony J. and Foot, Hugh C. (Eds.)
    1977   *It's A Funny Thing, Humour*. Oxford: Pergamon Press.

Clifton, Rodney A. and Roberts, Lance W.
    1993   *Authority in Classrooms*. Scarborough: Prentice Hall Canada Inc.

Cousins, Norman
    1979   *An Anatomy of an Illness*. New York: W.W. Norton & Company, Inc.

    1989   *Head First: The Biology of Hope*. New York: E.P. Dutton.

Damico, Sandra Bowman and Purkey, William W.
    1978   "Class Clowns: A Study of Middle School Students." *American
            Educational Research Journal*, Vol. 15, No. 3, pp. 391-398.

Damico, Sandra Bowman
    1980   "What's Funny About a Crisis? Clowns in the Classroom." *Contemporary
            Education*, Vol. 51, No. 3 (Spring), pp. 131-134.

Dardick, Geeta
    1990   "Learning to Laugh on the Job." *Principal*, Vol. 65, No. 5, pp. 32, 34.

Denscombe, Martyn
    1980   "Pupil Strategies and the Open Classroom." Pp. 50-73 in Peter Woods
            (ed.) *Pupil Strategies: Explorations in the Sociology of the School*.
            London: Croom Helm.

Dodge, Bernard J. and Rossett, Allison
    1982   "Heuristics for Humor in Instruction." *NSPI Journal*, May. Pp. 11-14,
            32.

Dubrerley, W.
    1988   "Humour as Resistance." *International Journal of Qualitative Studies in
            Education*, Vol. 1, No. 2, pp. 109-123.

Earls, Patricia L.
    1972   "Humorizing Learning." *Elementary English*, Vol. 49, pp. 107-108.

Eble, Kenneth Eugene
    1967   *A Perfect Education*. New York: The Macmillan Company.

Fine, Gary Alan
    1977   "Humour in Situ: The Role of Humour in Group Culture." Pp. 315-318 in Chapman, Antony J. and Foot, Hugh C. (Eds.) *It's A Funny Thing, Humour*. Oxford; Pergamon Press.

Fuchs, Estelle
    1969   *Teacher Talk*. Garden City, N.Y.: Doubleday.

Giddens, Anthony
    1986   "Action, Subjectivity, and the Constitution of Meaning." *Social Research*, Vol. 53, pp. 529-545.

Gilliland, Hap and Mauritsen, Harriett
    1971   "Humor in the Classroom." *Reading Teacher*, Vol. 24, pp. 753-756.

Glaser, Barney G.
    1978   *Theoretical Sensitivity*. Mill Valley, California: Sociology Press.

    1982   "Generating Formal Theory." Pp. 225-232 in Robert G. Burgess (Ed.) *Field Research: A Source Book and Field Manual*. London: George Allen & Unwin.

Glaser, Barney G. and Strauss, Anselm
    1967   *The Discovery of Grounded Theory: Strategies for Qualitative Research*. Chicago: Aldine Publishing Company.

Goldstein, Jeffrey H.
    1976   "Theoretical Notes on Humor." *Journal of Communication*. Vol. 26, No. 3., pp. 104-112.

Goodchild, Jacqueline D.
    1959   "Effects of Being Witty on Position in the Social Structure of a Small Group." *Sociometry*, Vol. 22, pp. 261-272.

Goodman, Joel
    1983   "How To Get more Smileage out of Your Life: Making Sense of Humor, then Serving It." Pp. 1-21 in Paul E. McGhee and Goldstein, Jeffrey H. *Handbook of Humor Research*, Vol. II Applied Studies. New York: Springer-Verlag.

Goodson, Ivor and Rob Walker
    1991   "Humour in the Classroom." Pp. 28-43 in Ivor F. Goodson and Rob
                 Walker (eds.), *Biography, Identity & Schooling: Episodes in Educational
                 Research.* London: The Falmer Press.

Graeven, David B.
    1975   "College Humor in 1930 and 1972: An Investigation of Using the Humor
                 Diary." *Sociology and Social Research*, Vol. 59, No. 4, 406-410.

Grotjahn, Martin
    1957   *Beyond Laughter.* New York: The Blakiston Division, McGraw-Hill.

Hammersley, Martyn
    1981   "Ideology in the Staffroom." Pp. ??? in Barton, L. and Walker, S. *School
                 Teacher and Teaching.* Brighton, Falmer Press.

    1984   "Staffroom News." Pp. 203-214 in Andy Hargreaves and Peter Woods
                 (Eds.), *Classrooms & Staffrooms: The Sociology of Teachers & Teaching.*
                 Milton Keynes: Open University Press.

Hargreaves, David
    1978   "Whatever Happened to Symbolic Interactionism?" Pp. 7-22 in Barton,
                 Len and Meighan, Roland (Eds.) *Sociological Interpretations of Schooling
                 and Classroom: A Reappraisal.* Nafferton, Driffield, England: Studies in
                 Education, Nafferton Books.

Hewitt, John P.
    1976   *Self and Society: A Symbolic Interactionist Social Psychology.* Boston:
                 Allyn and Bacon, Inc.

Hewitt, John P. and Hewitt, Myrna Livingston.
    1986   *Introducing Sociology: A Symbolic Interactionist Perspective.* Englewood
                 Cliffs, New Jersey: Prentice-Hall.

Hill, Deborah J.
    1988   *Humor in the Classroom: A Handbook for Teachers (and Other
                 Entertainers).* Springfield, Illinois: Charles C. Thomas.

Horn, Gunnar
    1972   "Laughter: A Saving Grace." *Today's Education*, Vol. 61, pp. 37-38.

Jansen, Golie and Peshkin, Alan
    1992   "Subjectivity in Qualitative Research." Pp. 681-725 in Margaret D.
            LeCompte, Wendy L. Millroy and Judith Preissle (eds.) *The Handbook of*
            Qualitative Research in Education. San Diego: Academic Press, Inc.

Kambouropoulou, P.
    1930   "Individual Differences in the Sense of Humor and Their Relations to
            Temperamental Differences." *Archives of Psychology*, Vol. 19, No. 121,
            pp. 5-77.

Kaplan, Robert M. and Pascoe, Gregory C.
    1977   "Humorous Lectures and Humorous Examples: Some Effects upon
            Comprehension and Retention." *Journal of Educational Psychology*, Vol.
            69, No. 1, pp. 61-65.

Keenan, Diane
    1985   "Economics with a Sense of Humor." *Social Studies Review*, Vol. 24
            (September). Pp. 22-26.

Koller, Marvin R.
    1988   *Humor and Society: Explorations in the Sociology of Humor.* Houston:
            Cap and Gown Press, Inc.

Korobkin, Debra
    1988   "Humor in the Classroom: Considerations and Strategies." *College*
            Teaching, Vol. 36, No. 44 (Fall). Pp. 154-158.

Krogh, Susanne
    1985   "He Who Laughs First: The Importance of Humor to Young Children."
            Early Child Development and Care. Vol. 20, pp. 287-299.

Kuhlman, Thomas L.
    1984   *Humor and Psychotherapy.* Homewood, Ill.: Dow-Jones-Irwin.

Leacock, Stephen
    1937   *Human and Humanity: An Introduction to the Study of Humour.* London:
            Thornton Butterworth, Ltd.

Leone, Robert E.
    1986   "Life after Laughter: One Perspective." *Elementary School Guidance &*
            Counselling. December, pp. 139-142.

LeCompte, Margaret D. and Preissle, Judith
  1993   *Ethnography and Qualitative Design in Educational Research* (Second
          Edition). San Diego: Academic Press, Inc.

Martin, Wilfred B.W.
  1982   *Teachers' Pets and Class Victims.* St. John's: Publications Committee,
          Faculty of Education, Memorial University of Newfoundland.

  1983   *Helpful, Understanding and Cooperative Teachers.* St. John's:
          Publications Committee, Faculty of Education, Memorial University of
          Newfoundland.

  1984   "Student Perceptions of Teachers' Pets-Class Victims Phenomena."
          Canadian Journal of Education/Revue Canadienne de l'education. Vol. 9,
          No. 1, pp. 89-99.

  1985a   *Student Views on Schooling in Newfoundland and Labrador.* St. John's:
          Publications Committee, Faculty of Education, Memorial University of
          Newfoundland.

  1985b   *Student Embarrassment.* St. John's: Publications Committee, Faculty of
          Education, Memorial University of Newfoundland.

  1985c   *Voices from the Classroom.* St. John's: Creative Publishers.

  1987   "Students' Perceptions of Causes and Consequences of Embarrassment in
          the School." *Canadian Journal of Education/Revue Canadienne de
          l'education.* Vol. 12, No. 3, pp. 277-293.

Martin, Wilfred B.W. and Baksh, Ishmael J.
  1984   *Student Observations on School Rules in Newfoundland and Labrador.* St.
          John's: Publications Committee, Faculty of Education, Memorial
          University of Newfoundland.

  1987   *Factors Relating to Student Input Into Teaching.* St. John's: Publications
          Committee, Faculty of Education, Memorial University of Newfoundland.

Martin, Wilfred B.W. and Spain, William
  1986   *A Comparative Analysis of Student Views on Schooling: A Question of
          School Size.* St. John's: Background Report No. 2, Small Schools Project,
          Government of Newfoundland and Labrador.

Martineau, William H.
    1972   "A Model of the Social Functions of Humor." Pp. 103-114 in J.H. Goldstein and P.E. McGhee (eds.), *The Psychology of Humor*. New York: Academic Press.

Masten, Ann S.
    1986   "Humor and Competence is School-Aged Children." *Child Development*. Vol. 57, pp. 461-473.

McGhee, Paul E.
    1974a   "Cognitive Mastery and Children's Humor." *Psychological Bulletin*. Vol. 81, pp. 721-730.

    1974b   "Moral Development and Children's Appreciation of Humor." *Developmental Psychology*. Vol. 10, pp. 514-525.

    1976   "Development of Humor Response: Review of the Literature." *Psychological Bulletin*. Vol. 76, pp. 328-348.

McGhee, Paul E. and Chapman, Anthony J. (Eds.)
    1980   *Children's Humour*. Chichester: John Wiley and Sons.

McLaren, Peter
    1986   *Schooling as a Ritual Performance: Towards a Political Economy of Educational Symbols and Gestures*. London: Routledge & Kegan Paul.

McMorris, Robert F., Urbach, Sandra L., and Connor, Michael C.
    1985   "Effects of Incorporating Humor in Test Items." *Journal of Educational Measurement*, Vol. 22, No. 2 (Summer), pp. 147-155.

Mead, George Herbert
    1929   "The Nature of the Past." Pp. 235-242 in J. Coss (Ed.), *Essays in Honour of John Dewey*. New YorK, Henry Holt.

    1934   *Mind, Self and Society*. Chicago: University of Chicago Press.

Mealyea, Robert
    1989   "Humour as a Coping Strategy in the Transition from Tradesperson to Teacher." *British Journal of Sociology of Education*. Vol. 10, No. 3, pp. 311-333.

Mindess, Harvey
    1971   "The Sense in Humor." *Saturday Review*, August, P

Nilsen, Don L.F.
1993   *Humor Scholarship: A Research Bibliography*. Wesport, Connecticut: Greenwood Press.

Nilsen, Don L.F. and Nilsen, Alleen Pace
1982   "An Exploration and Defense of the Humor in Young Adult Literature." *Journal of Reading*. October, pp. 58-65.

Parsons, Jim
1977   "Competency-Based Teacher Education Module No. 2499 On Classroom Humor." *Contemporary Education*. Vol. 48, No. 2, pp. 110-111.

Peterson, Ivars
1980   "Humor in the Physics Classroom." *The Physics Teacher*, Vol. 18, No. 9 (December). Pp. 646-650.

Pollard, Andrew
1979   "Negotiating Deviance and 'Getting Done' in Primary School Classrooms." Pp. 75-94 in Barton, Len and Meighan, Roland (eds.) *Schools, Pupils and Deviance*. Driffield: Nafferton.

Ransohoff, R.
1975   "Some Observations on Humor and Laughter in Young Adolescent Girls." *Journal of Youth and Adolescence*. Vol. 4, pp. 155-170.

Rogers, Carl
1969   *Freedom to Learn*. Columbus, Ohio: Charles F. Merrill.

Rogers, Vincent R.
1984   "Laughing With Children." *Educational Leadership: Journal of the Association for Supervision and Curriculum Development*. Vol. 41, No. 7 (April), pp. 46-50.

Salameh, Waleed Anthony
1983   "Humor in Psychotherapy: Past Outlooks, Present Status, and Future Frontiers." Pp. 61-88 in McGhee, Paul E. and Goldstein, Jeffrey H. (Eds.) *Handbook of Humor Research* (Vol. II, Applied Studies). Springer-Verlag: New York.

Sluder, Alice Wilde
1986   "Children and Laughter: The Elementary School Counselor's Role." *Elementary School Guidance & Counselling*. December, pp. 120-127.

Smith, R.E., Ascough, J.C., Ettinger, R.F., and Nelson, D.A.
    1971   "Humor, Anxiety, and Test Performance." *Journal of Personality and Social Psychology.* Vol. 19, pp. 243-246.

Stebbins, Robert A.
    1974   *The Disorderly Classroom: Its Physical and Temporal Conditions.* (Monographs in Education No. 12). St. John's: Faculty of Education, Memorial University of Newfoundland.

    1975   *Teachers and Meaning: Definitions of Classroom Situations.* Leiden: E.J. Brill.

    1980   "The Role of Humour in Teaching: Strategy and Self-Expression." Pp. 84-97 in Peter Woods (ed.) *Teacher Strategies: Explorations in the Sociology of the School.* London: Croom Helm Ltd.

Sudol, David
    1981   "Dangers of Classroom Humor." *English Journal* (October), pp. 26-28.

Tattum, Delwyn P.
    1982   *Disruptive Pupils in Schools and Units.* London: Wiley.

Terry, Roger L. and Woods, Margaret E.
    1975   "Effects of Humor on the Test Performance of Elementary School Children." *Psychology in the Schools.* Vol. 12, No. 2 (April), pp. 182-185.

Townsend, Michael A.R. and Mahoney, Peggy
    1981   "Humor and Anxiety: Effects on Class Test Performance." *Psychology in the Schools.* Vol. 18, pp. 228-234.

Walker, Rob
    1991   "Classroom Identities." Pp. 7-27 in Ivor F. Goodson and Rob Walker (eds.), *Biography, Identity & Schooling: Episodes in Educational Research.* London: The Falmer Press.

Walker, Rob and Clem Adelman
    1976   "Strawberries." Pp. 133-150 in Michael Stubbs and Sara Delamont (Eds.) *Explorations in Classroom Observations.* London: John Wiley.

Walker, Rob and Goodson, Ivor
    1977   "Humour in the Classroom." Pp. 196-227 in Peter Woods and Martyn Hammersley (Eds.) *School Experience.* London: Croom Helm.

Waller, Willard
    1965   *The Sociology of Teaching*. New York: John Wiley & Sons, Inc.

Weaver, Richard L.
    1982   "Positive Qualities of the Large-Group Lecturer." *Focus on Learning*, Vol. 8, pp. 10-13.

Weaver, Richard L. and Cotrell, Howard W.
    1987   "Ten Specific Techniques for Developing Humor in the Classroom." *Education*, Vol. 108, No. 2, (Winter), pp. 167-179.

Weiss, M. Jerry
    1981   "The Serious Nature of Humor." *English Journal* (October), pp. 72-74.

Willis, Paul
    1977   *Learning to Labor: How Working Class Kids get Working Class Jobs*. New York: Columbia University Press.

Woods, Peter
    1976   "Having a Laugh: An Antidote to Schooling." Pp. 178-187 in Martyn Hammersley and Peter Woods (Eds.) *The Process of Schooling: A Sociological Reader*. London: Routledge and Kegan Paul.

    1983   "Coping at School Through Humour." *British Journal of Sociology of Education*, Vol. 4, No. 2., pp. 111-124.

    1984   "The Meaning of Staffroom Humour." Pp. 190-202 in Andy Hargreaves and Peter Woods (Eds.), *Classrooms & Staffrooms: The Sociology of Teachers & Teaching*. Milton Keynes: Open University Press.

    1986   *Inside Schools: Ethnography in Educational Research*. London: Routledge & Kegan Paul.

    1990   *The Happiest Days? How Pupils Cope with School*. London: The Falmer Press.

    1992   "Symbolic Interactionism: Theory and Method." Pp. 337-404 in Margaret D. LeCompte, Wendy L. Millroy and Judith Preissle (eds.) *The Handbook of Qualitative Research in Education*. San Diego: Academic Press, Inc.

Zielger, Virginia, Boardman, Gerald, and Thomas, Donald M.
    1985   "Humor, Leadership, and School Climate." *The Clearing House*. Vol. 58, No. 8 (April). Pp. 346-348.

Zinger, David J.
    1985   "The Functions and Factors of Humour in Counselling." Unpublished Master of Education thesis in Educational Psychology, Winnipeg, Manitoba: University of Manitoba.

Ziv, Avner
    1976   "Facilitating Effects of Humor on Creativity." *Journal of Educational Psychology.* Vol. 68, No. 3, pp. 318-322.

    1983   "The Influence of Humorous Atmosphere on Divergent Thinking." *Contemporary Educational Psychology.* Vol. 8., pp. 68-75.

    1984   *Personality and Sense of Humor.* New York: Springer.